"*Fed Up with Flat Faith* is just the ticket for a turnaround. . . . We're given tools to help us get to that place where we allow the Holy Spirit to work in us. We can find ourselves living the way we've always wanted to live, accomplishing the things we were meant to accomplish. From flat to totally pumped — get ready for a faith inflation!"

— RHONDA RHEA, radio personality, humor columnist, author of nine books, including *Espresso Your Faith*

"If you are fed up with your flat faith, like I was, let me recommend this simple but powerful book. The stories will encourage you, the biblical teaching will feed your soul, and the OK-so-here's-what-you-do wisdom will get you moving from flat faith to fired-up faith."

— CONNIE CAVANAUGH, speaker and author of *From Faking It to Finding Grace* and *Following God One Yes at a Time*

OTHER NEW HOPE BOOKS
by Kathy Howard

Before His Throne:
Discovering the Wonder of Intimacy with a Holy God

God's Truth Revealed:
Biblical Foundations for the Christian Faith

Unshakeable Faith:
8 Traits for Rock-Solid Living

Fed up with

FLAT FAITH

✝

*10 Attitudes and Actions
to Pump Up Your Faith*

kathy howard

NEW HOPE
P U B L I S H E R S
Gospel-Centered. Missions-Driven.

BIRMINGHAM, ALABAMA

New Hope® Publishers
P. O. Box 12065
Birmingham, AL 35202-2065
NewHopeDigital.com
New Hope Publishers is a division of WMU®.

Library of Congress Cataloging-in-Publication Data
Howard, Kathy, 1961-
  Fed up with flat faith : 10 attitudes and actions to pump up your faith / Kathy Howard.
    p. cm.
  Includes bibliographical references.
  ISBN 978-1-59669-367-8 (pbk.)
  1. Boredom--Religious aspects--Christianity. 2. Christian life. 3. Mediocrity. 4. Spiritual formation. I. Title.
  BV4599.5.B67H69 2013
  248.4--dc23
                          2012035895

Cover and Interior Design: Glynese Northam

ISBN-10: 1-59669-367-3
ISBN-13: 978-1-59669-367-8

N134110 • 0313 • 3M1

DEDICATION

With much love to my parents
Ray and Margaret Head
From the beginning you pointed me to Christ

ACKNOWLEDGMENTS

God has blessed my life with precious, fiery-faithed friends: Susan, Lisa, Connie, Jan, Stephanie, and Pattie. Your example and encouragement have sparked my own faith. Thank you for your friendship and for allowing me to share a part of your journey in this book.

A special thanks to Dr. Steven Brown. Steve, your input and insight were invaluable to this project.

Thanks to Randy Bishop, who gave me the push I needed to write this book.

My sincere appreciation to Andrea Mullins, Joyce Dinkins, and the staff at New Hope Publishers for your commitment to Christ and to spreading the good news through the written word.

TABLE OF CONTENTS

INTRODUCTION

Does your faith feel tired and dry? Do you lack a sense of real connection with God? Do you desperately desire to be desperate for God?

Many Christians struggle with flat faith. They long to experience passion and excitement in their Christian life, but nothing they do seems to make a difference. I know what that's like, because I've been there. But I didn't have to settle for flat faith and neither do you.

You cannot set your faith on fire. Only God can create a roaring blaze. However, you can obediently position yourself where God can do His work.

How can this book help? It doesn't merely describe the problem and show you glimpses of fiery faith. This book gives you practical steps for following God out of flat faith to a place where He can set your faith on fire. These steps are not guaranteed, instant fixes. But they are foundational spiritual truths and faith principles that we Christians often lose sight of.

We will explore five attitudes and five actions that can prepare your heart and life for God's work. These ten practical, biblical steps of faith will shift your attitude and change your behavior to put you in the center of God's activity. These steps do not guarantee you will never again experience periods of flat faith; even the most passionate believers have times of spiritual lows. But once armed with these biblical truths, you can stay close to God, always ready to receive what He wants to give you.

The "Questions for Reflection and Discussion" section includes chapter-by-chapter questions that can be used for personal reflection or in small-group discussion. Maybe you know other Christians who are struggling too. Whether this will be an individual journey or friends will be joining you, it will be worthwhile. Are you ready to finally leave your flat faith behind?

PART ONE

†

MISSING SOMETHING

Chapter 1

FED UP

told her things I had always been too afraid to tell anyone before. *My faith felt dead. I doubted my salvation. God seemed so distant.* I saw something in Susan's life that I longed to have in mine. Her faith was vibrant and real. Even the way she talked about God demonstrated a dynamic in her relationship with Him that I lacked. I had been a Christian since childhood. I was active in church. I said and did all the right things. I even taught Sunday School. But my face never lit up when Jesus was the topic of conversation.

Wayne and I met Susan and her husband at church. We regularly spent time with them and several other young couples. From the beginning, I recognized Susan had something I desperately wanted. For instance, she turned to God first in every situation. I asked God for help only if I couldn't take care of it myself. Susan communicated with God constantly like He was a real person. My prayertime and Bible reading were dry and perfunctory.

I had wanted to ask Susan about her faith for a while, but that particular day was the first opportunity I had to talk to her alone. Both young mothers, we planned a play date for our toddlers. While the little ones played on the floor, I tearfully shared with Susan the doubts that had plagued me for nearly two decades. She listened with compassion, but she also challenged me to not be content with my condition.

Now that I had acknowledged to a Christian sister that something was wrong, my lifeless faith wasn't a secret anymore. I could not deny it. Finally desperate enough for God, I had

13

become vulnerable—with a friend and with God. Fed up with my dull, flat faith I could allow God to work. My friend did not "fix" me that day, but our encounter jump-started my journey toward a fiery faith. Along the way, God shifted a few of my attitudes and changed some of my actions to fire up my faith. God can use these same attitudes and actions to start a flame in your life.

Countless Christians experience flat faith. Many—even many who attend church regularly, minister to others, and teach Bible study—long to find excitement in serving Jesus, but continue to struggle. Some, who are discouraged, walk away from church altogether, while others simply settle for this dry ritual of faith. Still others keep searching for the kind of faith Jesus promised—full, abundant, overflowing! (See John 10:10.) That kind of faith is anything but flat!

The word *flat* can be defined as "without vitality or animation; lifeless; dull."[1] Many Christians with flat faith love Jesus and continue to serve Him, but they often feel as though they're simply going through the motions of Christianity. Their love for Christ is short on passion. They serve Him and His church largely out of a sense of duty or because that's what they've always done. The routine of the Christian life may even feel superficial and directionless.

Some believers have *never* experienced a vibrant faith characterized by real intimacy with Christ. Flat faith is all they've ever known. Others, like my dear friend Connie Cavanaugh, were once on fire for Christ but ended up spending a season in a spiritual wilderness. In her book, *From Faking It to Finding Grace,* Connie bravely tells her story of spiritual dryness. This pastor's wife once passionately shared her faith and lovingly ministered to her family, church members, and neighbors. As she served them, their pain always became her pain too. Finally, overwhelmed, Connie shut down spiritually and emotionally. She "faked it" for a decade, pretending everything was fine to her friends, her family, and her church. After ten years of wearing a spiritual mask, God graciously and lovingly began to show her the way out of that spiritual wilderness.

Does either of these scenarios even remotely describe your life? Do you long for more in your relationship with Christ? Do you crave the abundant life He promised? Fiery faith is not only possible, God wants it to be yours. God never intended for our life of faith to be boring and cold. You *can* connect with God in real ways. You *can* experience His activity in and around you. Your life *can* bear fruit that lasts.

Age-Old Problem

Flat, dry faith is not a recent phenomenon or a product of our contemporary culture. This problem plagued mankind long before the children of Israel grumbled in the wilderness. As far back as Genesis we can spot flat faith in the midst of God's people. Sarah, Abraham's wife, displayed symptoms of flat faith. She believed in God. She even left home with her husband to backpack over to Canaan. But Sarah's relationship with the Creator lacked a couple of vital elements. She did not expect God to work, and she did not believe He had the power to do what He promised. Both of these "symptoms" result from an insufficient knowledge of God. Sarah needed to get to know her Creator.

When Abraham came home with the news that God promised to give him offspring as numerous as the stars, Sarah set about to make it happen with the help of her Egyptian maidservant. Rather than letting God work His plan in His way, she tried to do it for Him in a way that made sense to her. Years later, when God's messenger made it clear yet again that God's plan included Sarah, she laughed because it seemed impossible to her. Sarah's limited knowledge *of* God limited what she believed *about* God. Sadly, she lived her faith without any expectation of or trust in God's miraculous activity.

Martha, our favorite New Testament hostess, suffered from her own consequences of flat faith. Activity replaced a vibrant relationship with her Savior. While Mary, her sister, sat at Jesus' feet and soaked up His teaching, Martha busily prepared the guest room and cooked a gourmet meal. *Serving* Christ distracted her from *enjoying* Christ's presence (Luke 10:38–42). Martha was too busy to spend time fostering intimacy with Christ. On a positive note, Scripture shows us that Martha's relationship with Jesus grew. After the death of Martha's brother, Lazarus, she makes an incredible declaration of faith in Christ. "I believe you are the Christ, the Son of God, who was to come into the world" (John 11:27). And this was before Jesus raised Lazarus from the dead. Obviously Martha had spent some quality time with Jesus.

We could visit many more examples of flat faith in Scripture. The Bible beautifully preserved stories for us from both ends of the faith spectrum. The passionate and the passionless. Those who lived with purpose and those who lacked purpose. Those with a deep connection to their heavenly Father and those who felt disconnected.

Eli and Samuel, in the Old Testament Book of 1 Samuel, exemplify this contrast. Eli was from the tribe of Levi, a priest of the Most High God, a descendent of Aaron. Eli ministered at God's Tabernacle all his life. God had chosen the Levites from all the tribes of Israel to be His priests, to burn incense in His presence, and to offer sacrifices for the people. For 40 years Eli led Israel to worship and serve the Lord. Eli was a chosen man of God, a leader of God's people. But as we will see shortly, Eli's *religiosity* hindered his *relationship* with the living God.

Samuel was a boy from the tribe of Ephraim. His mother, Hannah, suffered with infertility for many years before God answered her prayers and blessed her and her husband with baby Samuel. To fulfill her vow of dedication, when Samuel was still very young—probably around three years old—Hannah took him to Eli. There Samuel stayed to learn from Eli his mentor and to grow "up in the presence of the LORD" (1 Samuel 2:21).

Samuel thrived both physically and spiritually. He grew "in stature and in favor with the LORD and with men" (1 Samuel 2:26). In fact, during this period of Israel's history when "the word of the LORD was rare" (1 Samuel 3:1), God spoke directly to Samuel. First Samuel chapter 3 records that the LORD was with Samuel as he grew up. He let none of Samuel's words fall to the ground, and God revealed Himself to Samuel through His word. Samuel enjoyed a full, dynamic relationship with God.

The biblical account clearly shows that Eli's faith was dramatically different from Samuel's. Samuel's vibrant, intense faith fostered a life that was open and responsive to God and His activity. Eli's dutiful, routine faith left a spiritual hole in both his life and his family's life that paved the way for heartbreak.

Our very first encounter with Eli in Scripture demonstrates his lack of sensitivity to spiritual things. As Hannah poured her heart out in prayer to God in front of the Tabernacle in Shiloh, Eli mistakenly assumed she was drunk. He failed to recognize intense, fervent prayer and missed the presence and activity of God.

Eli's two sons were "wicked men" who had "no regard for the LORD" (1 Samuel 2:12). Hophni and Phinehas, treated their priestly ministry with contempt by using their position to satisfy their physical cravings. As High Priest, Eli had the responsibility to prevent this abuse of power. Instead, he ignored his sons' behavior because their temporal pleasures meant more to him than God's honor. By failing to intervene, Eli condoned their sin and dishonored his holy God. The result? God took the lives of Hophni and Phinehas in battle and declared that Eli would be the last old man in his family line. Eli's flat faith profoundly affected those closest to him.

Let's look at one last thing from Eli's life. To me, this may be the saddest result of flat faith. Eli did not hear God speak. Although he had served in the Tabernacle for decades, God chose to speak to the young boy, Samuel, instead of the experienced priest.

What can you and I learn from this ancient Israelite priest and a young Ephraimite named Samuel?

1. Flat faith derails God's purposes for our lives.
2. We don't have to settle for flat, dry faith.

God wants us to experience a vibrant, fulfilling relationship with Him. If we simply go through the motions of faith, at best we miss out on the abundance of all God has planned for us. And at the worst, our apathy can have far-reaching consequences.

I'd like to read a record of Eli in his early days to know what brought him to where we find him in 1 Samuel. Did he begin his life as a priest with excitement? Did things happen along the way that seemed to throw cold water on the fire of his faith? Perhaps. Maybe what happened to Eli is what I see happening to Christians in churches today.

Eli came from a family of priests. His father was a priest and his grandfather was a priest. Essentially, Eli had served God since the day he was born. His faith was expected and routine. It's just what he did. He probably never thought about doing it any other way. Eli believed in God. He wanted to experience Him in a fresh and dynamic way, but his habit of faith got in the way. I can relate.

I've Been There

I started in the middle of my story; now let's go back to the beginning. I was a "church baby." From infancy my parents faithfully took me to Sunday School, worship service, Vacation

Bible School, and Wednesday nights. I memorized Bible verses, earned high attendance pins, and wore wire hanger angel wings covered with gold garland in the Christmas pageant. I went to church camp and sang in the youth choir.

At eight years old I accepted Jesus as my Savior. I clearly remember the day when I realized I was a sinner in need of forgiveness. I understood what Jesus accomplished for me on the Cross. I can still see myself sitting in a straight-backed wooden chair across the desk from our pastor, talking through these things while my mother hovered in the doorway. I became a baby Christian that day.

For the next 18 years nothing much changed. I still claimed Christ as my Savior, but I also remained a spiritual babe. I remained active and involved in church. I followed all the rules and did all the right things. In fact, my brother sarcastically called me "Sister Mary Kathryn." And although Mary Kathryn is indeed my given name, I'm sure my parents never meant it to be used as a synonym for Miss Goody Two-Shoes.

Even with all my church activity and right living, I experienced little to no spiritual growth. The rich relationship I wanted with Christ eluded me. Something vital was missing. Connected to church, I still felt disconnected from God. I had no real sense of God's presence.

If a world record existed for the most "rededicated" Christian, I would definitely be a contender. Countless times, during my teen and early adult years, I traipsed down the aisle or bowed my head in prayer to dedicate my life to Christ yet again. Although I accepted Jesus as my Savior at an early age, for almost two decades I struggled to sense God's presence. I could see the kind of faith I longed to have in other's lives. God seemed so personal to them; they enjoyed an intimacy with Christ I envied. Despite my weak attempts for a fresh start with Jesus, my faith remained dry and stale. Many times I wondered, *What is wrong with me?*

My faith languished even more during my college years. After a few futile attempts to find a church and get involved in campus ministry, I gave up. Soon after college graduation, Wayne and I married and found a church home in our new city and got involved. Looking back, I know that, for me at least, it was more because I thought we *should* than because I *wanted* to. My church activity resumed, but my faith remained flat, dull, and lifeless.

God's Divine Intervention

Then came that day with Susan. The day that desperation gave way to vulnerability. Fed up and tired of trying to ignite my faith through my own works and activity, I humbly admitted I could not do it. Honesty with myself, Susan, and ultimately God opened the way for His activity. *I* could not make myself into what God wanted me to be. *I* could not find the abundant life Jesus promised. But God could do it all.

Shortly after my conversation with Susan I joined a ladies' Bible study group for the first time. Through the Book of Romans, God showed me things in His Word I had never really seen before. For the first time in all my churchgoing years I finally understood that my salvation and my faith have nothing to do with me and everything to do with Christ.

Now, you may be asking, "How did you miss *that*!?" Bear with me just a minute and I'll try to explain. Intellectually, I knew the facts. Christ must be my Savior *and* my Lord. God saved me for a purpose—to lay down my life and obediently follow Jesus. My life is not my own, I've been bought and paid for with the blood of Christ. I knew all these things, but still I missed the point. I spent almost two decades armed with the knowledge of the faith God intends. Like Eli, I simply went through the motions of faith.

I attended church; I served in a ministry position; I read my Bible and prayed. But everything was powerless, stunted, boring. Flat. Like Martha, sometimes the busyness of faith hindered me from finding the relationship with Jesus I craved. Many times I thought: *Since I already do "all the right things," then this must just be it for me. Some people are just wired to be more spiritual than others. I will just be happy with what I have.* Sadly, I was also like Sarah. I did not know God well enough to believe He could—and would—act in my life.

Thankfully God used the power of His Word to correct my faulty thinking. Here are a few things He taught me right away:

- Nothing about my faith is about me; everything is about Him and for His glory.
- I have no power to make myself grow spiritually; but God does and it's His job.
- The relationship with Jesus is primary; good works and church activity flow out of this relationship as I obey Him.

His correction and redirection immediately started my faith in a new trajectory. I began to hunger for God's Word; I started growing spiritually; and I even wanted to tell others about Jesus. Throughout the rest of this book we will explore the attitudes and actions that will position you before God so He can fire up your faith. Since God broke through to my heart all those years ago He has done a lot of work on me. But there is so much refining still to do.

Still Growing

I have certainly not become all God wants me to be. "Mountaintop" experiences are not a daily occurrence! My spiritual "feelings" continue to ebb and flow. However, now, a sense of God's presence and an excitement in serving Him is the norm for me instead of a rare—or never—occurrence.

In fact, many of our biblical heroes display a passion for Christ

I long to share. For instance, David's longing for God is evident in both his writing and in the record of his life. We know from Scripture that David sinned. His passion for God did not make him perfect, but it did keep him coming back to the One who offered forgiveness. I believe David's relentless and passionate pursuit of the Father is why God described him as a "man after his own heart" (1 Samuel 13:14).

My favorite expression of desire for Christ in Scripture comes from the Apostle Paul. I have committed this passage to memory because I long to share Paul's intensity in my pursuit of Christ.

> *But whatever was to my profit I now consider loss for the sake of Christ. What is more, I consider everything a loss compared to the surpassing greatness of knowing Christ Jesus my Lord for whose sake I've lost all things. I consider them rubbish, that I may gain Christ and be found in him, not having a righteousness of my own that comes from the law, but that which is through faith in Christ — the righteousness that comes from God and is by faith. I want to know Christ and the power of his resurrection and the fellowship of sharing in his sufferings, becoming like him in his death* (Philippians 3:7–10).

Paul's intense longing for Jesus charted the course of his life. Christ's calling filled each moment with relevance. Although Paul lacked material belongings, he was rich. Paul suffered in prison for the sake of the gospel, but he was freer than most people. And when Paul endured one hardship after another, he rejoiced that the power of God would be displayed through his weakness.

We could use many words to describe Paul's faith. *Zealous. Fiery. Intense. Inspiring. Significant. Meaningful.* But *flat*? Never.

Paul's life displayed passion and purpose in abundance! Do you ever look at some of the great people of God in the Bible and wonder, *How do I get some of that?*

Are You Fed Up?

Do you struggle with finding real passion and purpose in your relationship with Christ? Like Sarah, do you expect too little from God? Perhaps like Martha, you are too busy with the works of faith to foster your relationship with Jesus. Maybe like Eli you simply go through the motions of faith. Even if you don't experience the same tragic results, the loss is still great.

How do you know if your faith needs a boost? If the title of this book captured your attention, that's a good indication you're already looking for more. If you feel like you've simply been doing church and have missed out on an active relationship with a real Person, then keep reading. You can also take a quick faith inventory. Below is a list of characteristics, derived from Scripture and my own experience, that indicate your faith is more routine than robust.

- Relationship with Christ is not deepening and growing
- Religious activities overshadow your relationship with Christ
- Life of faith feels boring, tired, or overwhelming
- Feeling of disconnect from God; no real sense of His presence
- God seems silent
- Little excitement over or awareness of God's activity
- Little or no anticipation that God will work
- Dry, forced worship; praising and acknowledging God's nature do not come easy
- Little or no personal worship outside of corporate worship; you rarely find yourself spontaneously worshipping God
- Nagging sense you should be experiencing more in your relationship with God

- Notice fiery faith in others' lives that you desire
- Efforts and activity produce few results of eternal value

Perhaps a few—or many—of these could be used to describe your faith. Do you want more? Do you want to experience the full life of faith that Jesus offers? You don't have to settle for flat faith. You don't have to give up or pretend. God wants to replace your flat faith with fiery faith!

I want to emphasize one important truth: We cannot grow our own faith. From beginning to end, faith is strictly God's work. We can't even muster up faith to believe in Jesus. God gives us our faith (Ephesians 2:8). And only God's Spirit can change, grow, and transform our faith (2 Corinthians 3:18; Colossians 1:29). But God expects our cooperation. He calls for our active and obedient participation in His work in our lives (1 Corinthians 9:24-27; 1 Timothy 4:7; Philippians 3:12-14). That's the purpose of this book—to learn to position ourselves before God so He can accomplish in our lives the things that only He can accomplish.

This book highlights key attitudes and actions found in Scripture that help God's people position themselves for Him to work in their lives. The truth principles may challenge you. They still challenge me! Much of what's in this book you may have heard before, particularly if you've been in church many years. If you're anything like me, you probably *know* a lot that you never *apply*. That was why my faith was flat for so long. I pray that this time God will help you apply His truths to your life.

Are you ready to be vulnerable? Remember, you can't do it, but God can. Perhaps some of your Christian friends or family members have faith with those qualities you desire. They can be an invaluable source of encouragement and prayer. Ask one or more to partner with you as you seek to cooperate with God in your faith transformation.

Chapter 2

GATHERING TINDER

Jan is an average gal with an above average passion for Jesus. When she talks about Him, her eyes widen, her voice fills with excitement, and sometimes she even has trouble standing still. God has gifted Jan with a beautiful voice she uses to serve Him. When she lifts it in praise, her love for Him is obvious. In those moments, Jan's worship fuels worship in the hearts of many around her. Others long to have the passion for Jesus they see in Jan, but it eludes them. And a few simply watch and listen, seemingly unmoved.

How would Jan's worship affect you? Would your ready heart quickly warm in worship? Would you struggle to find passion for the One who made you? Or would you be like the few — resigned to settle for a listless, boring faith?

When the topic of Jesus comes up around my friend Jan, she either beams with excitement or cries tears of joy and gratitude. What about you? How do you react when you hear the name "Jesus?" Perhaps a smile tugs at the corners of your mouth and your heart warms within your chest. "Jesus." Or maybe you feel apathetic or detached. "Jesus."

In chapter 1, we visited a few biblical characters that lacked passion and purpose in their relationship with God. Here's a quick reminder:

- Sarah's insufficient knowledge of her Creator failed to produce trust in His character or an expectation of His activity.

- Martha's busyness left her no time to foster intimacy with Jesus.
- Eli substituted religious activity for a vital relationship with God.

For decades, I identified with Sarah and Martha and Eli. I struggled to find a way to start a faith fire in my cold heart. Trying to ignite my faith myself simply led to one failure after another. Discouragement and hopelessness were the only results. As I shared in the first chapter, nothing changed until I became vulnerable before God and desperate enough to allow Him to do His work in my life.

You don't have to settle and you don't have to constantly struggle. Although even the most passionate Christian occasionally feels cold, that does not have to be the default setting in your relationship with Jesus. God can replace cool distance with warm intimacy and a fiery passion. You can have a "fired-up" faith!

The slang phrase *fired up* means to be thrilled, excited, and enthusiastic. Your faith can be fired up! You *can* let go of your flat, dry faith and embrace the faith God calls you to possess. God can replace your apathy with an intense craving for Him. He can set your faith on fire.

Recalling experiences with God can act as tinder for His fire. I must admit, I know very little about building an actual fire. However, according to experts, "tinder" is the first and most important material needed in building a fire because it ignites so easily.[1] Touched by even a slight spark, these small pieces—such as wood, leaves, or straw—quickly catch fire, providing the flame needed to light the kindling and in turn the larger wood. A roaring fire begins with the small tinder.

"Tinder experiences" include times we sensed God's presence, saw Him work in our own lives or the lives of others, and those moments when our hearts were overwhelmed with awe and worship for our Creator. As we recall these experiences, we are gathering tinder that God can ignite. The more experiences we gather, the more we will desire to experience. As our craving for God increases, we will recognize more of His activity. As we recognize more of His activity, these experiences continue to build our passion and increase our craving still more. It's a glorious, faith-building cycle. Let's see how this works in our lives by considering our appetites, looking at a biblical example, and then gathering our own bundle of tinder.

Avoid Substitutes

In her best-selling book *Made to Crave*, Lysa TerKeurst says God made us to crave. "Yes, we were made to crave—long for, want greatly, desire eagerly, and beg for—God. Only God." God created within us a passionate desire for something beyond ourselves—an intense longing that only a passionate pursuit of Him can ultimately satisfy. Unfortunately, we too often try to satisfy our God-given, passionate craving with something else.

For many years Lysa's substitute was food. For others, the substitute may be money, a career, children, or other relationships. No substitute will ever permanently quench our spiritual longing for God. Only an intimate, passionate relationship with our Creator can fully and completely fill us up to overflowing.

Lysa also says, "We crave what we eat." The more we partake or experience God, the more we will desire Him. We won't be able to get enough of Him. Experience with Him fuels our passion. Someone with a fiery passion for God will be satisfied in Him yet always seeking more of Him. Author A. W. Tozer calls this the "soul's paradox of love." (By the way, Tozer wrote this long before the Newsboys sang it.) King David is the ultimate biblical example of this kind of unquenchable longing for God. Although David had found God, he continued to pursue Him.

David's Fiery Passion

Expressions of David's fiery faith fill the psalms. In times of trouble, celebration, and repentance David voiced the true craving of his heart—to stay intimately connected to His God. David's desire for God consumed him. In the Sixty-third Psalm, He compared his longing for His maker to the need for water in the desert.

> O God, you are my God; I earnestly search for you. My soul thirsts for you; my whole body longs for you in this parched and weary land where there is no water (Psalm 63:1 NLT).

Have you ever experienced extreme thirst? Although I have never been lost in the desert without a canteen or nearby oasis, I have had times of intense thirst. Prolonged yard work in the heat of a Texas summer. Two days of labor accompanied only by ice chips. The aftermath of a 24-hour stomach bug. In those times, getting my hands around a big glass of icy cold water consumed my thoughts. Nothing else seemed important at the time. Satisfying my thirst was the only thing that mattered.

David longed for God like my body ached for water. Sufficient water quenched my physical thirst. Once fully hydrated, I could put the glass down and walk away. However, the more David experienced God, the more deeply he longed for Him.

> I have seen you in your sanctuary and gazed upon your power and glory. Your unfailing love is better than life itself; how I praise you! I will praise you as long as I live, lifting up my hands to you in prayer. You satisfy me more than the richest feast. I will praise you with songs of joy (Psalm 63:2–5 NLT).

When David witnessed Yahweh's glory, power, and holiness, he yearned to see more. When David felt the expressions of God's love for him, he ached to feel it again and again. Each time David lifted his voice in praise, his lips became more accustomed to worship.

David did not confine his worship to "church." He did not keep his relationship with God filed away in the "religious" section of his life. Thoughts of God flooded every corner. David's need for God overrode every other need.

> *I lie awake thinking of you, meditating on you through the night. Because you are my helper, I sing for joy in the shadow of your wings. I cling to you; your strong right hand holds me securely* (Psalm 63:6–8 NLT).

What comes to your mind when you wake in the middle of the night? I must admit, although I usually pray when I wake in the middle of the night, it's not thoughts of God that *keep* me awake. The thoughts that cause sleep to hide are often filled with worry and anxiety. David not only thought of God when he woke, but he also purposefully stayed awake to contemplate God and His ways. This conscious contemplation of God fostered a deep dependence in David. He diligently pursued God. His soul clung to Him in good times and bad because David had witnessed God's faithfulness.

This "clinging" reminds me of the way Mark, my youngest child, used to wrap himself around one of my legs and sit on my foot. As he clung tight, I could walk around the house, carrying him along every step of the way. It was almost impossible to pry him loose. Oh, that our souls would always cling to God like that!

But where do we start? Let's look back again at David. David put more value on his relationship with God than he did his own life. He recognized the superiority of God's love because he had received it. When David recalled his experiences with God he naturally responded with worship. As he worshipped, David encountered God again. And once again, David's appetite for Yahweh grew.

My craving for sweets mirrors this on a superficial level. When I pass up chocolate, ice cream, cookies, or candy for a while my desire for them wanes. I actually get along just fine without them. But if I have a taste—say, even just one small bite of chocolate—then I want more. In fact, the more sugar I consume, the more I want. Even when I am full, I long to experience the creamy sweetness on the roof of my mouth.

The best way to break my craving for sweets is to stop eating them. When I deny myself, after just a little while I forget how truly great the treats taste. My desire for sugar continues to lessen with time. The quickest way to develop my sweet tooth is to keep slurping up the sugary treats. One bite is so good, it leads to another. Two bites dictate a third. Once that indulgent taste is in mouth, it seems I just cannot get enough. In a similar way, I can either fuel or smother my passion for God. If I want my faith to remain dull and lifeless, then I limit the time I spend with Him. I will keep God at arm's length. But if I want to increase my desire for Him, I will position myself to experience Him over and over.

Gathering Tinder

David's experiences with God acted like tinder to fuel his faith fire. When he recalled feeling God's presence, or remembered witnessing His glory, he naturally responded with passionate worship. When David contemplated God's character and His past help, David's trust in and dependence on God was fortified and strengthened.

We have access to the same kind of tinder in our relationship with God. Recalling our past experiences with Him can lay a combustible foundation for the Holy Spirit's spark. We will gather some tinder together in a moment. Then, in later chapters, we will pile on some attitudes and actions that the Holy Spirit can use as kindling to start a roaring blaze. *(Remember what we talked about in the last chapter: Only the Holy Spirit can transform our faith, but we can obediently position ourselves to be in the center of His activity.)*

In the chapters ahead we will explore five life-changing attitudes and five key actions that the Holy Spirit can use to set our faith on fire. But, let's do a little tinder gathering for our faith fire right now by reflecting on our past experiences with God. Just as David's faith was fueled by remembering his divine encounters, your faith can be sparked by recalling those moments you felt God's presence, saw His activity, or were struck by His holiness.

You may feel as though you don't even have any tinder to gather. Perhaps you rarely, if ever, sense God's presence or see His activity. Be encouraged; if you are a child of God, He *is* with you. His presence is not based on our feelings, but on His promises. And God is always faithful to keep His promises.

- *I am with you always, to the very end of the age* (Matthew 28:20).
- *Never will I leave you; never will I forsake you* (Hebrews 13:5).

In the midst of my flat faith years, I did not feel the presence of God. I did not see His activity around me. But today, as I look back on those same years, I can see God's hand. He was there working in my circumstances and constantly turning my heart back to seek Him. He protected me from physical harm more than once. He obviously guided the course of my life to bring me to where I am today. If you are a believer in Jesus Christ, God *has* been active in your life even if you did not recognize it at the time.

In their insightful best-selling book *Experiencing God,* authors Henry Blackaby and Claude King help readers recognize God's activity. They emphasize that God is always at work around us and identify some things Scripture says only God can do:[2]

- God draws people to Himself.
- God causes people to seek after Him.
- God reveals spiritual truth.
- God convicts the world of guilt regarding sin.
- God convicts the world of righteousness.
- God convicts the world of judgment.

If you see any of these things happening around you, know that God is at work. If a lost friend or neighbor asks you about your faith in Jesus, that is God working in her life. If you feel compelled to repent of a sin or are convicted of disobedience toward God, that is God actively working on your heart. If you read the Bible and gain fresh understanding, or clearly see how a passage applies to a current situation in your life, that is God's Spirit revealing spiritual truth to you.

In those times when God seems distant or inactive, I remind myself of a time when I was keenly aware of His presence and activity. I recall an occurrence that caused me to stand in awe of His love or worship His majesty. This could be from my own life or divine activity in another's life that God allowed me to witness. For instance, reflecting on Victor's story always helps renew my confidence in the intimate, miraculous involvement of the Creator in our lives.

When I met Victor in his early 20s, his spiritual condition could be described as somewhere between atheist and agnostic. As a child, his father had taught him that God and eternity did not exist. He was told that this life was all there was so he'd better get everything out of it he could. But after testing this philosophy through his teen years, Victor's restless heart would not allow him to fully embrace it. He longed for more.

Victor's girlfriend, a brand-new Christian, urged him to join her in a Bible study I was leading for spiritual seekers and new Christians. Because of the changes he had already witnessed in Chelsey's life, he agreed, but his expectations were low. Then the teachings of Jesus caught Victor by surprise. Different from anything he had heard before, God's truth began to feed his spiritual hunger.

Over the course of two years, God continued to woo Victor. Slowly, God opened his mind to the truth of Christ and removed the spiritual calluses on his heart. In God's timing, Victor gave his life to Jesus. God allowed me and my husband the exciting privilege of leading him in that prayer of surrender.

Did you spot God's activity in Victor's life? If you need to, glance back at that list from *Experiencing God.* God drew Victor. God caused Victor to seek after Him. God gave Victor spiritual understanding. God convicted Victor of his need for a Savior. God transformed Victor's life. Within months, the live-for-the-moment party boy was preparing to lead a volunteer missions team on a two-week trip to Ukraine. Now that is something only God can do!

Personally witnessing a spiritual birth like Victor's confirms God's ever-present activity in this world. He continues to work in Victor's life. He has—and is—working in my life. And whether you are aware of it or not, God *has been* and *is* working in and around your life. He *is* present with you. Let's work together right now to identify some of those moments.

Striking a Spark

Prayerfully consider the prompts listed below. Take your time as you move through the list. Use the margin of this book, your journal, or a separate piece of paper to write down the specific instances in your life that God brings to mind. With each "God encounter" you remember, also record how you felt, how you responded (or should have responded), and what this instance teaches you about God and His ways. Recall times when:

- God strengthened or comforted you in a time of difficulty
- God provided for you in a time of material need
- God convicted you of sin to bring you to repentance and restore your relationship
- God allowed you to see Him working around you in circumstances or people's lives
- God overwhelmed you with the beauty and majesty of His creation
- God whispered guidance to your heart and mind
- God helped you understand and apply His Word
- God gave you a real and immediate sense of His presence
- Any other experience with God that He brings to your mind now

Well, did God help you remember many things you had forgotten? This "taste," this reminder of what it feels like to experience God's presence, can jump-start your desire for more. Please don't worry if your list is short right now. We humans have short memories. We tend to forget these precious moments, these incredible encounters with the Creator God. But they are not lost. Continued reflection and a prayerful attitude before God can help you reclaim those divine encounters. Today is just the beginning.

Don't stop with this small exercise. Continue to watch purposefully for God's activity. Remember those things that only God can do. Keep your eyes open to His work around you and seek to be aware of His presence with you. Start a journal to record these things and reread it regularly. Keep adding tinder to your faith fire!

Are you ready to go from flat to fired-up? It's only fair to warn you now: Fiery faith is glorious, but risky. If you're willing to be stretched and challenged and exhilarated, you don't have to settle for flat faith. Those who do not want to be stretched or challenged or exhilarated should simply settle for their safe, but flat, faith. Fiery faith will take you places you never imagined you would go. It will cause you to abandon things you thought you could never do without. It will birth hope where once there was only hopelessness.

I want to share a prayer with you written by A. W. Tozer that seems very appropriate. This prayer can be found in *The Pursuit of God: The Human Thirst for the Divine*. Make this your heart's cry to God as you begin this journey toward fiery faith.

O God, I have tasted Thy goodness, and it has both satisfied me and made me thirsty for more. I am painfully conscious of my need of further grace. I am ashamed of my lack of desire. O God, the Triune God, I want to want Thee; I long to be filled with longing; I thirst to be made more thirsty still. Show me Thy glory, I pray Thee, that so I may know Thee indeed. Begin in mercy a new work of love within me. Say to my soul, "Rise up, my love, my fair one, and come away." Then give me grace to rise and follow Thee up from this misty lowland where I have wandered so long. In Jesus' name. Amen.[3]

PART TWO

✦

ATTITUDE ADJUSTMENT

Chapter 3

INSIDE OUT

Attitude #1: Relationship over Religion

When I was a girl, our family life and schedule revolved around church. We attended Sunday School and worship service every Sunday morning. After lunch and a few hours of playing or reading at home, we all bounced back to church for the Sunday evening service. We gathered for prayer meeting on Wednesday nights. Fridays and Saturdays also often brought an additional activity or fellowship or missions project. Church service and attendance wove through the fabric of our family. The question of whether or not we would go on any given Sunday was never raised because we were a church family. This faithful commitment to church hindered my faith.

Please don't misunderstand me here. That last paragraph also describes my own family today, and I would not want it any other way. But there is a drastic difference between my childhood church attendance and my adult involvement. As a child, teenager, and even young adult, I attended church because that was what a good Christian girl was supposed to do. To me Christianity meant attending church, saying all the right things, and doing what everyone expected. Even though I had been *taught* differently, I *learned* that faith was what you do. I missed the part about it being all about Who you know.

Because I was practicing religion instead of living out a relationship with a Person, this church baby struggled to connect with the living God. Religion cannot satisfy. Unless our works of faith flow naturally out of a vital relationship with our Maker, it is merely religious ritual. We were created for relationship, not religion. By definition, *religion* refers to the external ceremonies and activities of worship—all those things we "do" to express our faith. As James said, faith that does not produce these kinds of works is dead and useless (James 1:20). But religious works performed only from a sense of duty or habit sap our spiritual strength, leaving our faith dry, weak, and flat.

Does this scenario describe you or your family? Like me, maybe you live in the "Bible Belt" of the United States. I grew up in northern Louisiana, smack dab in the middle of that strong church culture. In the 1960s and 1970s, attending church was not simply accepted, it was expected. "Good" people went to church and got involved. The majority of those attending truly had a relationship with Jesus. Their involvement in church was the result of that saving relationship. A few found that church met their social or business needs. Then others—like me—got lost in the "doing" of church and ended up only practicing religion. Some of these religious practitioners settled for these motions of faith. But I—and perhaps you—knew there was something more.

Although the Bible Belt culture of my childhood is less influential today, religiosity still hinders true relationship with Jesus. It seems that "doing" is a human's default setting. We like to make lists and check off the items, proving to ourselves that we have accomplished something. "Surely if I attend church, teach a Bible study class, and read my Bible every day then that will make things right between me and God." We can perform the outward motions of faith without actively pursuing the object of our faith.

Religion alone is as dry as yesterday's toast. But relationship with the living Savior is exciting, satisfying, and yes, passionate.

I have observed two types of this "inside-out" Christianity in the church—the kind of Christianity that puts the works of faith ahead of the object of our faith. We see both in Scripture. The first type is seen in individuals who desire to know God but have never entered into a saving relationship with Jesus Christ. They may have been in church all their lives, but somehow they missed the point of it all. Sadly, it happens so easily. The second type of "inside-out" Christianity is witnessed in those who once enjoyed a passionate love affair with Jesus but then allowed the busyness and activity of their faith to draw them into the "doing" of religion over the "being" of relationship. The first type needs to meet the Lord for the first time, while the second needs to make room in her calendar to foster the relationship with Him.

"What Must I Do?"

Even in the first century, sincere, devoted people missed the point of faith. Consider Nicodemus, the man we read about in the third chapter of John who came to see Jesus at night. Nicodemus was a Pharisee and a member of the Jewish ruling council. Not only was he a leader among the Jews, he was also highly knowledgeable regarding the Old Testament Scriptures and other religious writings. As a Pharisee, Nicodemus believed that strict obedience to God's law put you in right standing with Him. So I believe Nicodemus carefully followed each of God's commands as well as many religious customs and traditions established by men. But Nicodemus knew he was missing something.

I identify with Nicodemus because I've been there—trying to do all the right things, but still feeling disconnected from God. In desperation, I turned to a fiery-faithed friend who pointed me back to Jesus. Nicodemus secretly visited the Savior face-to-face. Under the cover of night, he sought out Jesus to get some answers—to discover why he lacked peace, satisfaction, and intimacy with God. He dared not ask his fellow Pharisees. "What would they think if they even suspected I have doubts? What would they do if they knew how I struggle?"

Many people in the church today hesitate to share their struggles and doubts with their friends and spiritual leaders. We feel the need to keep up appearances so everyone will think we have it all together. How Satan loves to trip us up with pride. It's his most-used tool. What we fail to realize is that our reluctance to seek help will keep us right where we are. God designed the body of Christ to encourage and build one another up. Step out and confess your need to a trusted, faith-filled friend.

Nicodemus took a small, but courageous step. He went to Jesus. Nicodemus began the conversation on safe ground. "Teacher," he said, "we all know that God has sent you to teach us. Your miraculous signs are proof enough that God is with you" (John 3:2 NLT).

Jesus wasn't fooled by Nicodemus's opening line. He knew exactly why he had come and what he needed. Religion was not enough for this highly respected religious leader. This Pharisee, this man who knew God's Word backward and forward, needed to be saved! Jesus responded, "I assure you, unless you are born again, you can never see the Kingdom of God" (John 3:3). If Nicodemus wanted to be child of God, a member of the King's household and a citizen of His kingdom, he had to be "born again."

Jesus was referring to a spiritual rebirth, not a physical one. Nicodemus was spiritually dead because of sin. He lacked the ability to relate to God, who is Spirit (John 4:24). Without being "born again" Nicodemus could never have a relationship with God.

Every person who has ever lived has this same problem. The Bible clearly shows that "all have sinned and fall short of the glory of God" (Romans 3:23). We have all chosen our own way over God's way. Granted, some of us have made this choice more often than others, but any and every sin is rebellion against our Creator. Sin, no matter how small or great the earthly consequences, brings spiritual death. "For the wages of sin is death" (Romans 6:23). This spiritual death cuts us off from God. And we can't do anything to restore the relationship. We can't go to church enough or perform enough good works. Every person — no matter how religious they may be — must be "born again" to "see the Kingdom of God."

To be born again means to be reborn spiritually. The Holy Spirit of God must give life to our sin-dead spirits. This happens by God's grace through a person's faith in God and trust in the sacrificial death of Jesus. Each of us has sinned and is under a penalty of spiritual death. But Jesus paid this penalty for us when He died on the Cross. If we trust in Jesus' sacrificial death to pay the penalty for our sin, God will graciously give us eternal life.

Easiest, Most Difficult Thing

Have you accepted this gift of salvation and entered into a relationship with Jesus? Receiving God's forgiveness and eternal life is the easiest, most difficult thing you will ever do. "Easy," because you don't have to do anything. God has already provided the payment for your salvation. "Difficult," because you can't do anything. Yet, that's exactly what our sinful, human nature wants — to do something.

Life has taught us that if we fail to act, we will usually have to give something up. If we fail to work, we won't have money to pay bills and buy necessities. If we fail to be a friend, we won't have the companionship of a friend. If we fail to love, we won't receive love.

If we fail to pay the electric bill, we won't enjoy light after sunset. These learned-by-experience principles, which truly apply to our physical world, can trip us up when it comes to salvation. We can't earn it or buy it. We can only receive what God freely gives.

Don't let a lifetime of religion hinder a true, saving relationship with Jesus. Perhaps God has shown you that you've been "doing" religion rather than "being" in a relationship with Jesus. Don't spend another day in the flat lands of religion. Be born again! (For more about how to have a relationship with Jesus, see appendix 2.) If today is your spiritual birthday, tell someone. Call a trusted friend or a minister at your church. Be vulnerable, reach out. Ask for their help to get growing in your new relationship with Jesus.

Lost Your First Love

So if good works can't save us, then why bother? Let's just sit around all day and visit with Jesus over coffee. While fostering our relationship with Jesus should be the priority for every Christian, God also has a specific purpose for each of us. We aren't saved *by* good works, but God saves us *for* good works.

> *Salvation is not a reward for the good things we have done, so none of us can boast about it. For we are God's masterpiece. He has created us anew in Christ Jesus, so that we can do the good things he planned for us long ago* (Ephesians 2:9–10 NLT).

God has a whole list of good works in mind for His children. When He saves us, He wants us to get to work on those things He has planned for us. We don't work for salvation, but we work as a result of our salvation. Good works should naturally and obediently flow from our lives as an overflow of our relationship with Jesus.

However, if we aren't careful, the relationship will take a backseat to the good works. Fostering and nurturing the relationship must come first. Remember, we have a "doing" nature. It is easy to allow our faith to become more and more about working and less and less about relating.

A friend of mine fell into the "doing" trap and let relating to her Savior fall by the wayside. Saved in high school, Carol loved Jesus and loved to use her gifts and talents to serve Him. For almost three decades she worked full-time, cared for her family, and served tirelessly in her church. Wherever a need popped up, Carol hopped to meet it. She had little rest or down time, but that was OK with her. Then a few problems cropped up at her church. A little gossip here. A hint of disunity over there. A bit of dissatisfaction in the back pew. There was even some complaining about Carol's work.

Soon Carol felt worn out and overworked. So she resigned from every position. But she didn't feel much better. So she backed off on attending church services too. Bitterness, disillusionment, and disappointment rushed in. Carol was burned out, not fired up. What happened to the passionate Christian, on fire for Jesus, and ready to take on the world?

Carol allowed her good works to become the driving force of her faith. Religion overshadowed her relationship with Jesus. When challenges came, Carol couldn't meet them. Distance from her Savior left her spiritually weak, overwhelmed, and ready to quit. She needed the strength, comfort, and guidance that walking closely with Jesus provides. The last time I talked with my friend, she was still smelling the smoke of burnout and struggling to reignite the fire of her faith.

Jesus expects our lives to produce good works, but He also knows that works can trip us up. We can get caught up in the doing and lose sight of being in relationship with Him. The church in Ephesus did this very thing. They "lost their first love." Paul wrote to the Christians in Ephesus between A.D. 55 and 60. In his letter, he reminded them that although they were saved by grace and "not by works, so that no one can boast," God also had good works for them to do, which He had "prepared in advance" (Ephesians 2:9–10).

The Ephesians took Paul's teaching about good works to heart. Their good deeds and hard work were well known. They persevered in the faith. They did not tolerate evil men. They endured hardship and did not grow weary in doing good. (See Revelation 2:2–3.) But somewhere along the way, their works supplanted their love for Jesus. They slipped into religion and sidelined relationship.

In the Book of Revelation, John records Jesus' words to the church in Ephesus. "You have forsaken your first love. Remember the height from which you have fallen! Repent and do the things you did at first. If you do not repent, I will come to you and remove your lampstand from its place" (Revelation 2:4–5). A few decades after the church learned that good works should be the natural overflow of their relationship with Jesus, we find they had allowed good works to take precedence over their love for Christ. Jesus did not condemn their works, but rather their motivation. The works themselves had taken first priority. Jesus called them to once again put Him first. Then the works would follow. Once again, we see how easy it is for religion" to replace relationship."

Busy and Proud of It!

We're up before the sun, pound the pavement or the keyboard all day long, and spend the after-work hours doing housework and helping with homework or cheering at ballgames and volunteering. Then we pass out from exhaustion only to get up and do it all over again. We're crazy busy and proud of it.

Our American culture values busyness. We tend to see a "busy" person as someone who is wanted, in demand, talented, and indispensible. Synonyms for the adjective "busy" include words like *industrious, diligent, persevering, energetic,* and *lively.* So in our minds, "busy" is good. Downtime is bad. Busyness has invaded our lives and become the way of life for most of us. We are too busy to simply hang out with our families. Too busy to go on a vacation. And definitely too busy to spend even a few minutes every day with God.

Our society has taught us to work at and even push the absolute limits of our time, resources, and physical ability. Usually, these limit-busters are positive, beneficial activities. But with all this good filling every nook and cranny of our lives, there is no room left for God's best. No space to respond when God calls us to a new task or shows us a need to be met or tells us to rest.

In his book *Margin,* Dr. Richard A. Swenson refers to this space we need in our lives as "margin." According to Swenson, relationships suffer the most in "marginless" living. Overly busy people are unable to "nurture and protect right relationships. . . . Margin, however, knows how to nurture relationships. In fact, margin *exists* for relationship."[1]

Dr. Swenson recognizes the spiritual impact of "marginless" living. "Chronic overloading also has a negative effect on our spiritual lives. We have less time for prayer and meditation, less energy for service, and less interest in relationship. If we don't move to establish effective priorities, overloading will continue to fill up our schedules and keep us captive. We must learn the art of setting limits."[2]

The sacred cow of busyness harms all our relationships. We need time for conversation, time to know and be known. We need "margin" for room to strengthen our relationships with our spouses, children, friends, and neighbors. More importantly, we need margin to deepen our relationship with God. Intimacy cannot be built through someone else's three-minute devotionals or distracted prayer while we drive to work. We must slow down, sit with God, talk to Him, listen to Him, and simply bask in His presence. When was the last time you did that?

I'm not saying you should delete all your appointments in Outlook or run your calendar through the shredder. Certain things *must* be done. Other things *should* be done. Still others *may* be done. Remember, God has planned good works for us to do. He wants us to enjoy life. But God also designed our bodies. He knows our limits. He recognizes that we need rest and refreshment and relationship. God is not the Author of burnout and "fast and furious."

We are too quick to add commitments to our lives and too slow about removing them. Each time God adds something new, we should consider if there is something that needs to be removed. When I was 40, God prompted me to enroll in seminary. I had three children at home and a host of church and community commitments. After prayerful consideration and consultation with the family we made some changes. God released me from one major ministry position. My two teenage daughters split the house cleaning duties. I let go of a few good things in order to add what God had decided was best.

Finding Margin

I challenge you to do something that could change your life, your relationships, and your faith. Are you sitting down? I challenge you to seriously evaluate the way you spend your time for the purpose of building margin into your life. Here are a few suggested guidelines:

- Start with prayer. Ask for God's guidance and wisdom as you seek to bring your life in line with His best.
- Involve your family. This won't help much without their support and participation. Explain what you are doing and why. Ask them to join you in adding "margin" to your life for the sake of you, your family, and your relationship with God. Your entire family could sit down together and prayerfully consider your commitments, including church activities.
- Make a list. Be thorough. Include daily, weekly, and monthly activities. Include your individual activities and those of your family — anything you do on a regular basis.
- Prayerfully let the list sit for a few days. Ask God to show you what things are from Him and what are not. Ask God to help you determine the limits of your time, resources, and energy.
- Discover your role in your local church. God *does* have a place of service for you in your local church, so ask Him where He wants you. God has put the body together just as He determines and you are a part. Just keep in mind He does not intend for you to be a foot *and* a hand *and* an eye *and* a toe *and* an elbow . . .
- Make cuts. Cut out activities and involvement as God directs. Unless God says otherwise, fulfill any commitments where people count on you, but do not volunteer for further service in that area.
- Set limits for yourself for future activities too. You might base limits on a number or amount of time. Set some limits on your children's activities too. Teach them now how to live life at God's pace, with plenty of room for Him.

Once you have created some margin, make a fresh commitment to make your relationship with God your first priority. This is an appointment you *should* have on your calendar every day. If you have fallen out of the habit of a regular quiet time, then you will need discipline to rebuild it. If your time with God has been rushed, commit to slowing the pace. Use some of that new margin to foster intimacy with God.

Right-Side Up

Inside-out Christianity lives religion over relationship. It's mostly public expression and little to no nurturing of relationship. We've seen two types of inside-out faith. First, we saw the kind that Nicodemus had—a man who still needed a saving relationship with Jesus. Then we considered the kind that my friend Carol slipped into. Once passionately in love with Jesus, she allowed good works to replace her intimacy with Him.

Is your faith inside-out? If you've never received Jesus as your Savior, do it today. If you've "forsaken your first love," repent. Don't turn your back on good works. Just make sure your works are the ones God has planned for you and not a myriad of others too!

There's a sweet spot of faith where we walk closely with Jesus and our lives produce the fruit of good works He desires. Jesus talked about this realm of abiding with His disciples on the night He was arrested. "I am the vine, you are the branches; he who abides in Me and I in him, he bears much fruit, for apart from Me you can do nothing" (John 15:5 NASB). When we maintain an intimate relationship with Jesus, He will guide us to the works He has planned for us and empower us to do them. Here are a few biblical suggestions to help you find your God-ordained place of service:

• Pray and seek godly counsel.
• Reflect on the passions and burdens God has placed on your heart.
• Consider your talents and spiritual gifting.

- Look back on the training and experiences God has used to equip you.

Find that sweet spot of faith and hunker down there. It's saturated with rest, refreshment, and relationship.

Chapter 4

WHO'S THE BOSS?

Attitude #2: Surrendered to the Savior

f *oxe's Book of Martyrs* sits prominently on my bookshelf. Written in the sixteenth century by John Foxe, stories of Christian martyrs fill its pages — men and women who willingly gave their lives rather than denounce their faith in Christ. Martyrdom did not end in Foxe's time. Estimates put the total number of Christian martyrs since the time of Christ at around 70 million. According to research cited by Italian journalist Antonio Socci, the rate of martyrdom increased in the last century. In his book, *The New Persecuted: Inquiries into Anti-Christian Intolerance in the New Century of Martyrs*, Socci says that 45 million — two-thirds of all Christian martyrs throughout history — died in the twentieth century.[1]

At least 70 million Christians have chosen death over life for the sake of Christ. Stephen, the first Christian martyr, was stoned outside the walls of Jerusalem (Acts 7:53) less than a decade after Jesus' resurrection. Stephen's death began a period of great persecution of Christians by the unbelieving Jews. In the A.D. mid-60s, martyrdom escalated under the Roman emperor Nero. Nero, infamous for his cruel creativity, threw Christians to the dogs, and used Christian believers as human torches, to light his garden parties.[2] Others, like Paul, lost their heads to the blade. Still others endured even more horrendous deaths. All this was merely the beginning of two millennia of martyrs.

From the time of Christ right up to today, Christians have been hated and hunted. The executioners and the methods of martyrdom may have changed, but the willingness of Christ followers to give their lives for Him never wavered. Their fiery passion for their Savior kept them clinging to Him even in the face of death. Why? Where did the courage come from to take this stand?

These Christians viewed their lives the same as did the Apostle Paul. "I have been crucified with Christ and I no longer live, but Christ lives in me. The life I live in the body, I live by faith in the Son of God, who loved me and gave Himself for me" (Galatians 2:20). Paul did not consider his life his own. It belonged completely to Jesus. God could do with it whatever He willed. It was His to use or use up for His glory. Can I say the same? Can you?

Come Out with Your Hands Up

My dad has always loved watching the old western movies, particularly those starring John Wayne. Some of the more repeated dialogue influenced my younger brother's playtime. He often demanded, "Come out with your hands up!" The "Marshall" wanted us "bad guys" to surrender. He expected us to throw up our hands and give ourselves over to his authority. My parents often played along, but I was too ornery.

Surrender. We sing about it in church, but do we really practice it? Do we even understand what it means to "surrender all?" Dictionary.com defines the verb *surrender* as "to give oneself up, as into the power of another; submit or yield."[3] I don't know about you, but I like to be my own boss, make my own decisions, and choose my own way. Giving up control is just plain hard. Seems silly though, doesn't it? Our God knows everything, has all power, and in reality is in control of everything. "Surrendering" is simply acknowledging and yielding to the authority He already possesses. Oh, so simple. Yet hard to do because of my stubborn, selfish nature.

Surrender marks the life of a true disciple of Jesus. The verse we read above from Galatians describes this kind of surrender. A disciple's sole desire should be to live for Christ, not herself. None of me and all of Him. A true disciple is sold out and on fire for her Savior. She follows His leading and obeys His commands, no matter how inconvenient or difficult. Fiery faith discards the "what's in it for me" mentality. I admit the apostle Paul did a much better job living this out than I do.

In the classic devotional book *My Utmost for His Highest*, Oswald Chambers elaborates on Galatians 2:20. "These words mean the breaking and collapse of my independence brought about by my own hands, and the surrendering of my life to the supremacy of the Lord Jesus . . . not following my own ideas, but choosing absolute loyalty to Jesus. . . . The passion of Christianity comes from deliberately signing away my own rights and becoming a bondservant of Jesus Christ."[4]

Did you catch that part about passion? Chambers said we will find passion in our relationship with Christ when we sign away our rights and become His bondservant. You won't find that on eBay. Our culture does not hold up dependence, submission, and subordination as ideals to attain. In fact, the opposite attitudes reign supreme. Independence, self-gratification, and me-first are king!

Why do we strive so hard to hang onto something that is not ours to begin with? We stubbornly insist on doing what we want the way we want to do it, forgetting that as God's children we have no rights of our own. "You are not your own; you were bought at a price. Therefore honor God with your body" (1 Corinthians 6:19–20). When God saved us, He purchased us from the masters of sin and death. The precious blood of Christ redeemed us from an "empty way of life" (1 Peter 1:18–19).

God knows what's best for you. He has a purpose for your life and He uniquely designed you to fulfill it. But only He can see the big picture. Only He knows the way you should go and the specific things you should do. Only in submission will you find the satisfaction, fulfillment, and abundance Christ promises. Will you yield to His authority? Will you come out with your hands up in surrender?

Scripture makes it clear that God calls us to let go and give everything over to the will and way of Jesus. Yet, still we often struggle to surrender. Let's take a look at two attitudes that keep us hanging on and then explore God's wonderful design for discipleship.

Consumer Christianity

I watched the tall buildings shake with the force of the earthquake. Fires broke out all along the street. Large chunks of concrete fell to the ground, smashing cars and other objects in their path. One building could not stand the stress and collapsed completely.

This might have happened in California, but my husband and I watched this particular scene unfold on the stage of a large church we visited near Houston. It had the feel and quality of a show at Disney World. Real fire. Real cars. Real expensive. And this church puts on similar productions each time the pastor kicks off a new sermon series.

Churches all over the country utilize similar methods to draw crowds to their services and keep them coming back. Their methods have been shaped by the power of the American shopper. Entertainment sells in our consumer-oriented culture. The consumer is king, so we give them what they want. The more lights, sound, flash, and razzle-dazzle, the better. Churches cater to the wishes and whims of the churchgoer so they don't go somewhere else. There's just one problem with all this: the consumer isn't king, Jesus is.

I realize this is an extreme example. But even the most faithful church or mature Christian can be influenced by the misguided values of our strong, consumer-oriented culture. Selfish desire can easily overshadow surrender. Unless we purposefully fight against it, our mass marketing society will produce Christian consumers who are weak disciples. At the worst, we hop from church to church in a selfish attempt to get the best program, the most charismatic preacher, or the newest facility. At best, we sometimes forget that Jesus is Lord and rather than "taking up our cross" daily and following His lead, we slip into consumer-mode and allow our own wishes and desires to call the shots.

Our self-serving culture repeatedly proves to be an "empty way of life" (1 Peter 1:18–19). Trendy clothes, a faster car, or the latest phone only pleases us temporarily. Soon we "need" the next latest and greatest. Human relationships are imperfect so we cast them away and try again. No one looks out for us, so we must look out for number one. This is the way the world attempts to find joy and satisfaction. Unfortunately, the me-first attitude bleeds over into our faith, warping it into something less than God intends: human-centered Christianity.

Our old selfish sin nature makes it hard enough to submit to the lordship of Christ. But when every other message we hear tells us to "have it your way" — "because you're worth it" — giving Jesus His rightful place is even more difficult. Instead of stoking the fires of our faith, seeking to satisfy our own desires is like throwing a bucket of water on the flames. To fully experience the abundant life Jesus promised, we must fully yield ourselves to Him. Unfortunately, consumer-oriented Christianity is not the only attitude that keeps us from complete submission.

First Things Second

Last Sunday, the preacher asked us to turn over our bulletin and number one to five down the left side of the page. Then he told us to list the most important things in our lives, writing down that thing we truly give top priority next to "number one." We all knew the *right* answer. But was it reality? Christians often have different answers to these two questions:

1. What *should* come first in my life?
2 What *does* come first in my life?

Three of the four Gospels tell us about a man who struggled with the answers to these two questions. This young, wealthy, influential "ruler" (Luke 18:18) had everything by the world's standards — money, youth, and power. But he came to Jesus in an attempt to find out if he was right with God.

"Good teacher," he asked. "What must I do to inherit eternal life?" Jesus entered the conversation at a comfortable place for the man. "If you want to enter life, obey the commandments" (Matthew 19:17). Following the rules of religion wasn't a problem for this particular man, so then Jesus cut to the heart of the matter.

"One thing you lack," He said. "Go, sell everything you have and give to the poor, and you will have treasure in heaven. Then come, follow me" (Mark 10:21). The young man couldn't do it. He wasn't willing to give up the one thing he valued more than God — his money.

In *Made to Crave*, Lysa TerKeurst reflects on this biblical encounter. "The rich young man then goes away sad because he won't give up the one thing that consumes him. He is so full with his riches he can't see how undernourished his soul is." TerKeurst also recognizes that different things consume different people. It isn't always money.

> *Jesus didn't mean this as a sweeping command for everyone who has a lot of money. Jesus meant this for any of us who wallow in whatever abundance we have. I imagine Jesus looked straight into this young man's soul and said, "I want you to give up the one thing you crave more than me. Then come, follow me."[5]*

What is that one thing you crave more than Jesus? That one thing that consumes you? Did something come to mind? The thing that takes first place in your life is your lord. That thing controls your time and attention. Money controlled the man who visited Jesus. He rejected the joy of true surrender in favor of slavery to worldly wealth. He wanted the salvation Jesus offered, but he wasn't willing to put Jesus first. This rich—but sad—young man failed to understand that yielding everything he had to Christ would bring him more than he could ever hope to gain from his riches.

Following the Leader

Whew! Total surrender to Christ. This may be a tough chapter for you to read. It's a tough chapter for me to write. "Surrender" is not a decision I make only once. I have to consciously keep coming back to surrender. I must yield to Jesus over and over because my sin nature wants to grab back control. This is God's design for discipleship.

God calls every Christian to total abandon, not just the "super spiritual." Surrender is not an item on the Christian menu we can order or leave off. Yet sometimes we eagerly accept Jesus as "Savior," drag our feet on the "lordship" thing, and are surprised when our lives do not reflect His power. Jesus willingly gave His life so we could be forgiven, but we hesitate to give ours to Him. If we have truly received forgiveness of our sin through the blood of Christ, then how can we have any response other than surrender to Him? When we take control of our lives, we are rebelling against His authority, and demonstrating our ignorance of the magnitude of His love.

You're reading this book because you want *everything* Jesus has to offer. Are you a true disciple of Christ, or have you surrendered to something else? If your faith has been flat—if like the rich young ruler you feel like you have been missing something—evaluate the condition of your "surrender." Let's see how God's Word defines it.

Jesus never watered down the reality of discipleship. He often used words of surrender to thin an obese crowd. Lots of people followed Jesus around, but far fewer were real disciples. Many were there for the show—the healings and other miracles—or what they thought Jesus could do for them. He fed the masses more than once! During one of those times when "large crowds were traveling with Jesus," He turned to them and said:

> "If anyone comes to me and does not hate his father and mother, his wife and children, his brothers and sisters—yes, even his own life—he cannot be my disciple. And anyone who does not carry his cross and follow me cannot be my disciple. Suppose one of you wants to build a tower. Will he not first sit down and estimate the cost to see if he has enough money to complete it?" (Luke 14:26–28).

In the first century, a disciple was not merely a student. A disciple also adhered to the teachings of his master. When Jesus spoke of discipleship, the crowds understood this. They knew if they wanted to be His disciple, they must submit to His authority.

Jesus does not hide any requirements. He also doesn't try to make discipleship appear easier than it is. Unfortunately, the church today often minimizes the cost of discipleship. Yet when we read Scripture there is no mistake: Following Jesus is costly and difficult.

This passage from Luke highlights at least four marks of a disciple of Jesus. If we desire to surrender all and follow the One who gave His life for us, we can check our lives for the following characteristics:

1. First Priority—Jesus must be more important than everything else in our lives, including family. The rich young ruler could not be Jesus' disciple because his money was his first priority. Jesus doesn't always ask us to give up those other things we hold dear, but sometimes He does.

2. Lifestyle—Discipleship is not just for Sundays or the 15 minutes we spend reading our Bibles in the morning. Jesus calls us to surrender every minute of every day. Surrender must also permeate every area of our lives—work, home, family, recreation, and church.

3. Obedience/submission—For Jesus, the Cross demonstrated His full and complete obedience to the Father. The cross Jesus calls His disciples to carry represents *our* total submission and complete obedience.

4. Conscious Choice—Jesus warned prospective disciples to "count the cost." Discipleship is serious business. Are we willing to pay the price of following Him? Unfortunately, many of us say no and miss out on the blessings of discipleship.

There Shall Be Showers of Blessings

Jesus asks much of His disciples, but He offers much more in return. "Truly I tell you," Jesus said to them, "no one who has left home or wife or brothers or sisters or parents or children for the sake of the kingdom of God will fail to receive many times as much in this age, and in the age to come eternal life" (Luke 18:29–30).

Jesus voiced this promise to His disciples right after that rich, young man sulked sadly away. Yes, discipleship is costly, but blessings beyond measure accompany surrender. Jesus promised abundance in this life and the next—heavenly reward and earthly recompense to those who leave all to follow Him. Matthew, Mark, and Luke all recorded Jesus' words of promise for those who surrender all for Him (Matthew 19:28–30; Mark 10:29–30; and Luke 18:29–20).

How should we understand this promise? All but one of the original apostles (not counting Judas the betrayer) were martyred for their faith. We know from Scripture and history that they never lived in opulence or acquired great fame and power. But they did receive Jesus' promise. Several decades after Jesus' death and resurrection, Peter taught believers to trust in and cling to the promises of God because Peter had learned God keeps His promises.

> *Simon Peter, a servant and apostle of Jesus Christ, To those who through the righteousness of our God and Savior Jesus Christ have received a faith as precious as ours: Grace and peace be yours in abundance through the knowledge of God and of Jesus our Lord. His divine power has given us everything we need for a godly life through our knowledge of him who called us by his own glory and goodness. Through these he has given us his very great and precious promises, so that through them you may participate in the divine nature, having escaped the corruption in the world caused by evil desires (2 Peter 1:1–4).*

God may indeed choose to use wealth, fame, or power in the life of one of His children, but He does not promise these things in exchange for obedient surrender. He does promise family, physical provision, eternal life, and persecution (Mark 10:30). Some new believers are disowned by their earthly families when they come to Christ. Jesus gives them a spiritual family, who will love, encourage, and support them. Some believers leave home and livelihood to follow Jesus to a missions field. Jesus meets their physical needs. Some believers suffer ridicule, alienation, and worse because of their faith. Jesus pours out peace, comfort, and strength. Christians who choose to live this life God's way instead of the world's way will experience peace, joy, fulfillment, spiritual transformation, and genuine fellowship in the community of God's people. But the greatest blessing is in knowing Christ more fully and deeply (2 Peter 1:3). Surrendered faith in Christ brings blessings the world cannot offer. These are the promises of surrender.

I Surrender All

Are your hands in the air yet? We don't have any negotiating power when it comes to surrender. It's a simple yes or no. Let's review the terms Christ has established.

> *Then he said to them all: "Whoever wants to be my disciple must deny themselves and take up their cross daily and follow me. For whoever wants to save their life will lose it, but whoever loses their life for me will save it. What good is it for someone to gain the whole world, and yet lose or forfeit their very self?" (Luke 9:23–25).*

- Deny self: Acknowledge that your life is not your own. You have been bought with a price and now belong to Jesus. He has the right to do with you whatever He chooses. Our relationships and possessions are not our own either. God calls us to "hate" (Luke 14:26) these things. "Hate" is simply an expression of contrast in comparison to our love for Jesus. Luke's use of the term "give up" (Luke 14:33) in the same passage helps us understand what Jesus asks of us. We may retain possession but Jesus has ownership.

We are simply stewards, holding them in trust, willing to part with them if Jesus asks.

- Take up your cross: God expects complete obedience no matter where He leads. For Jesus it meant death on a cross. We can learn God's general commands for all believers by studying His Word. For His specific will and direction for your life, stay in His Word, seek Him in prayer, and get godly counsel when needed.

- Daily: Jesus knew we would need to make a conscious choice to follow Him every day. Our stubborn, sinful natures constantly pull us toward rebellion. Let's choose Him today. And tomorrow. And the next day.

- Follow Him: Jesus is our King, Master, and Lord. He is the One worthy of our loyal devotion and obedience. We should be able to write "Jesus" next to number one on our priority list. Nothing else should compete for the spot.

Let's close this chapter with a prayer of commitment. If you are ready to surrender all to Jesus, then tell Him now. Feel free to use the prayer below if you'd like. I would also encourage you to sign your name and write the date at the bottom of the page. Then on one of those days when you feel a bit ornery and independent, you can remember the day of surrender.

✝

Jesus, You are my Savior and my Lord. You own me because You bought me with Your blood. You deserve all my allegiance and obedience. I put You first, denying my own will, wishes, and way. Use me or use me up for Your glory!

Chapter 5

CRAZY IN LOVE

Attitude #3: Remember Christ's Forgiveness

Picture a young couple newly in love. When they are together, everyone else fades into the background. They see only each other. Separation is almost physically painful. He consumes her thoughts and she consumes his. They long to please each other and the other's needs come first. Everything and everyone else takes second place to the object of their love. Longtime couples sometimes call them "giddy." They may even shake their heads and say, "Oh, this will pass." But secretly, they wish their own relationships still had the same passion.

New Christians experience a similar obsession with Jesus. Overwhelmed by His mercy and grace, captured by His love and forgiveness, new believers are "giddy" in their relationship with their Savior. Nothing else holds the same excitement. Brimming with unbridled devotion they want everyone to know what Jesus did for them. Their passion cannot be contained. Long-time Christians witness their excitement and say, "Oh, this will pass." And sadly, it often does.

Perhaps you experienced this in your own life. When you first received Christ, your loving enthusiasm for Him continually bubbled out, spilling onto those around you. But as the weeks and months passed, your relationship became less passionate and more routine. You were still committed to Christ, but the ardor you once felt for Him faded into a comfortable affection.

Where does this intense passion felt by new believers originate, and why does it so often fade? An individual comes to Jesus for salvation because she has recognized her need for a Savior. Keenly aware of her own sin, she humbly bowed before Christ and received the forgiveness that only God can offer. She responded to Christ's selfless sacrifice for her on the Cross with overwhelming gratitude and deep love. Unfortunately, over time she forgets the heinous nature of her sin. She fails to remember what *her* forgiveness cost *Jesus*.

Even longtime Christians can reignite our fiery passion for Christ and foster a deeper love for Him. We must remember. We must go back to the beginning of our salvation, contemplate our sin, and once again consider Christ's saving act for us. Then we must not forget. Regular reflection on the incredible truths of our salvation will help us fall in love with Jesus again and again. That's where I want to be — giddy in love with my Savior. How about you?

After a quick look at a biblical example of astounding love for Jesus, we will explore what the Bible says about the nature of our sin and the price it cost. Our goal is to gain a better understanding of the depth of what Christ did for us on the Cross to fire up our flat faith.

She Loved Much

Jesus once attended a dinner party at the home of Simon the Pharisee (Luke 7:36–50). Luke's story centers on a certain woman "who had lived a sinful life." When she learned Jesus was at Simon's, she could not stay away. While Jesus reclined on cushions beside the table, the weeping woman wet His feet with her tears and wiped them with her hair. Then kissing His feet, she lovingly anointed them with expensive perfume. She did not care what her actions looked like to others. Her love for Jesus made that inconsequential.

Simon, unmoved by the woman's passionate demonstration, silently questioned Jesus' authority and identity. Simon assumed Jesus must not be a prophet since He allowed this "sinful woman" to touch Him. Jesus knew exactly what Simon thought and took the opportunity to teach him—and us—an important spiritual truth.

Jesus told Simon a parable about two debtors who owed money to the same moneylender. One debtor owed a far greater amount than the other. When neither could pay, the lender canceled both debts. "Now which of them will love him more?" Simon rightly acknowledged that the man who owed the greater debt would respond to the lender with greater love. But he failed to recognize himself in Jesus' story.

The contrast between the woman's response to Jesus with that of Simon's is glaring. The woman loved Jesus so passionately because she realized the magnitude of His forgiveness on her behalf. Saved by her faith in Christ (see Luke 7:50), she responded to His abundant forgiveness with great feelings of gratitude and love. But Simon, who failed to recognize the depth of his need for Jesus, had no love for the only One who could provide forgiveness. Jesus summed it up nicely: "I tell you, her sins—and they are many—have been forgiven, so she has shown me much love. But a person who is forgiven little shows only little love" (Luke 7:47 NLT).

Simon was "forgiven little" not because he was not a sinner, but because he failed to acknowledge his sins and repent. He would not—and could not—love Jesus until he was struck by the truth of his sinfulness. Until that time, Simon would "love Jesus little" and respond to the sins of others with self-righteous indignation.

Much to Forgive

By definition, Christians have repented of their sins and received Christ's forgiveness. However, we often fail to recognize the depravity of our sin before our holy God. We tend to measure our sin against those around us instead of against the perfect, sinless Savior. The trouble with this standard of measurement is that we will always be able to spot someone who is a "greater sinner" than ourselves. "Oh yes, I need a Savior, but not near so much as my neighbor."

We are also prone to forget the price of our forgiveness. Eternal salvation costs *us* nothing. We receive it freely, as a gift of grace from a loving God. Yet the price was unbelievably high. Our salvation cost *God* everything. How soon we forget.

Before we can begin to appreciate the enormity of God's forgiveness we need to better understand the nature of our sin. Even then I don't believe we can come close to grasping the staggering scope of God's saving work on our behalf, but let's give it a try.

What is sin? Wayne Grudem, in his widely read book *Systematic Theology: An Introduction to Biblical Doctrine*, defines sin like this: "Sin is any failure to conform to the moral laws of God in act, attitude, or nature."[1] We humans sin by what we do, how we think, and even in who we are. Our actions, lack of actions, thought processes, motivations, and character all reveal us to be sinners. Before God does His sanctifying work in us, we are sinners, thoroughly and completely.

Notice that Grudem's definition clearly points out that sin is our failure to conform to God's laws. *God* is our standard. Not our neighbor. Not the laws of the land. Not the changing mores of our society. God created humans in His image. He made us to reflect His glory to the world. But sin has distorted the image of God in mankind as a whole and individually. You are a sinner. I am a sinner. No human but Jesus has ever escaped the grip of sin. *"For all have sinned and fall short of the glory of God"* (Romans 3:23).

The Bible uses the metaphors of light and darkness to depict the drastic chasm between God's holiness and humanity's sin. "God is light; in him there is no darkness at all" (1 John 1:5). Our holy God is "resplendent with light" (Psalm 76:4). God lives in "unapproachable light" (1 Timothy 6:16). God is totally holy in every way, completely without sin. Therefore He is totally light, completely without darkness.

Picture the brightness of the earth's sun in the sky. Now imagine how bright the light would become if you were able to move closer to the sun's surface. Soon only light would exist. All darkness and shadow would be gone. In Him is light; there is no darkness at all.

Now imagine the darkest place you've ever been. No street lights. No moon. No dim glow from a distant house. No hint of light from any direction. Those without God live in darkness like this. Before meeting Jesus, we too were separated from the Light. Our thinking was "futile and our foolish hearts were darkened" (Romans 2:21). Because we "loved darkness instead of light," because our deeds "were evil," we lived under God's condemnation (John 3:18–19).

The Bible paints a dark, distressing picture of our sin. Here is a summary of our condition without God:

- Our hearts are deceitful and desperately sick (Jeremiah 17:9).
- Even our "righteous" deeds are like filthy garments to God (Isaiah 65:6).
- None of us "does good" or seeks after God (Psalm 14:1–3).
- We are unable to come to Jesus on our own (John 6:44).

- We are slaves of impurity and lawlessness (Romans 3:18).
- Nothing good dwells in us (Romans 7:18).
- We cannot understand spiritual things (1 Corinthians 2:14).
- We are dead in our sin (Ephesians 2:1).
- We are objects of God's wrath (Ephesians 2:3).
- Our minds and consciences are defiled (Titus 2:15).

Sounds hopeless, doesn't it? In his letter to the Christians in Ephesus, Paul described their condition *before* salvation as "without hope and without God" (Ephesians 2:12 NLT). But the *after* picture is glorious: "But because of his great love for us, God, who is rich in mercy, made us alive with Christ even when we were dead in transgressions—it is by grace you have been saved" (Ephesians 2:4-5). Yes, our sin condition was hopeless until God demonstrated His love for us. While we still sinners—while we still lived in the depths of darkness of our own making—Jesus died for us (Romans 5:8).

From Darkness to Light

In John 3:16, the well-known verse about God's great gift, Jesus Himself points to God's love for the world as the motivation for our salvation. Because God loved us He gave us Jesus. Jesus did not come to condemn us. We were already condemned because of our sin. We "loved the darkness instead of light because our deeds were evil." But Jesus—God's light who came into the world—shone in the darkness and exposed our sin. Those who believe in Him step out of the darkness and into His marvelous light. (See John 3:16–21.)

In his letter to the Ephesians, Paul beautifully contrasts the depth of our sinful depravity with the gift of our eternal salvation. Before Christ saved us we were dead in our sin. We disobediently followed the ways of the world, and Satan was at work in us. Sin dictated our thoughts and desires. We satisfied the cravings of our sinful nature. Therefore, we were objects of God's wrath, deserving of eternal punishment. (See Ephesians 2:1–4.) Dark picture indeed.

But then God's loving light broke through. Because He loved us so much, God mercifully made us alive in Christ. By His grace, God saved us and gave us a place in the heavens with Christ. God did this so He could show us how gracious and kind He is to us through Jesus. We did not deserve this salvation. In fact, we could never do enough to earn it. It can only be received through faith as a gift from God. Our salvation is God's work from beginning to end. (See Ephesians 2:5–9).

We once walked in darkness, but now we are "light in the Lord" (Ephesians 5:8). This glorious gift from God cost us nothing. But our salvation was not without a terrible price. The wages of sin is death (Romans 6:23). Without the shedding of blood there is no forgiveness for sin (Hebrews 9:22). But *our* life did not purchase our salvation. Our forgiveness was not secured through the shedding of *our* blood. No, Jesus Christ obtained our eternal redemption with *His* blood (Hebrews 9:12). He gave *His* life to pay the price of our sins (Romans 5:6–8).

How should we respond to this sacrifice of love? Just like that "sinful woman," who showed up at Simon's house—with unabashed gratitude and love. Let's throw away all sense of decorum and just love Jesus like crazy. Without limits or embarrassment. Let's be vocal, unafraid to tell others about why we love Him so. Does that sound odd? Maybe it does because we don't regularly see this kind of behavior in Christians. An exuberant show of love for Jesus may be unusual in many Christian circles, but for my friend Stephanie it's as normal as breathing.

Crazy in Love with Jesus

Stephanie's "before Jesus" story is a difficult one. So I'd like you to hear the majority of it in her words:

> I didn't begin life as a sweet, planned, little bundle of joy. My mom was raped and I was the result. Two wonderful parents adopted me, loved me, and raised me as their own. But from the age of three until about the age of twelve, two extended family members repeatedly raped and molested me. That abuse shattered and skewed my concept of love.

Stephanie's painful childhood experiences shaped her teen and early adult years. She made a series of wrong choices that took her further and further away from God.

> I became pregnant at 17. The father and I married, but by the age of 19, I was divorced and a single mom. I spent the next five years "looking for love in all the wrong places"—which is exactly how I met my husband in a bar. He was the drummer in the band. Our life together was a reflection of the whole rock and roll band scene. Not a pretty picture. But then no picture is pretty without God in the middle of it.

Stephanie seemed to be running away from God as hard as she could. But our loving God intercepted her. He used a television evangelist to share the gospel message with her for the first time. Then over the course of two years, He continued to whisper words of love to her heart. Finally, in God's time, Stephanie entered into a love relationship with Jesus.

It was a sweet October day in 1987 when Jesus reached down, captured my heart and life and radically changed this broken girl with a bad past and a bleak future. Jesus loved me just as I was. With all my failures. Even with all my sins He loved me so much that He died for me. I didn't have to prove my love for Him, I just had to accept His love for me.

I experienced what it means to be "born again." That's exactly what I was . . . brand new . . . born again by the Great I Am. Sin became something I not only noticed in my life, but for the first time it grieved my heart to grieve His. God's Word nourished me more than food. It consumed and changed me. Time in God's Word and in prayer fostered within me a deep love for Him. I became increasingly passionate about living for the Living God.

Six months after Stephanie became a Christian, God also saved her husband. God gave them a heart for missions and sent them to Costa Rica for three years. Now back in the United States, Stephanie's husband serves on a church staff and Stephanie teaches God's Word through writing and speaking to women.

Stephanie's overflowing, obsessive love for Jesus marks her life and ministry. No one misses the obvious truth that she lives for Him. If you ask Stephanie why she is so crazy about Jesus, she will tell you.

I love Him because He loves me. I can't get over that! He loves me with this perfect, relentless, love that causes me to cling to Him. He is my very breath; He is my reason for living. This world offers nothing that even comes close to what He gives. I know because I have tried so many other things and found they left me empty every time. I'm also well acquainted with love gone wrong and perverted relationships. Only Jesus could change my heart and life . . . and I can't forget what He has done for this wretched soul. I'm so thankful that He was willing to take my place and redeem my soul at such great a cost. It's impossible to express what He has done because of His love for each of us. All I know is I love Him like crazy and I long to make my life one big "thank you" for all He has done for me. He is all I need and I desperately want my life to say, "I love You back!"

Stephanie has struggled over if, when, and how to share her story. It's hard to tell and hard to hear. She doesn't want to sensationalize it or use it to draw attention to herself. But she also does not want to waste what God has done in her life. So she tells her story to bring glory to God and to encourage His people. Stephanie's life has been messy, partly due to the sin of others. But she also quickly acknowledges the mess was compounded by her own sin and foolish choices.

Many Christians have pasts filled with heartache and sin. Stephanie's story shows how God delights in forgiving, restoring, and loving those of us who are sinful, broken, and unlovable — which we all are without Christ. She includes herself among those who have "been forgiven much" and is so thankful that her past no longer defines her and holds her captive. Christ has set her free. Stephanie actively demonstrates how we can respond to God's saving work with abundant gratitude, joy, and love. She is truly crazy in love with her Savior. And her passion is contagious.

Remember When?

Your life before Jesus does not have to be as dramatic as Stephanie's to fall head over heels in love with your Savior. Every person has sinned against the holiness of God. Each of us deserves nothing less than eternal death and separation from Him. Therefore, every Christian has more than enough reason to be passionately in love with the One who died to supply their forgiveness.

Overwhelming gratitude and love are normal and appropriate responses to the gift of salvation God has given us. Unfortunately, those of us who have been redeemed by the blood of Christ tend to allow our passion for Him to wane over time. The further we get from that day in our own history when God saved us, the dimmer the memory becomes of exactly what He saved us from and to.

We also tend to forget that God continues to extend His grace to us after our salvation. Christians may be forgiven, but we still sin. Although God's goal for us is that we sin less and less as He transforms us into the image of Christ, we will not be perfect this side of heaven. Therefore, we need God's forgiveness and grace on a regular basis. This means we should be regularly responding with gratitude and love.

Since it's so easy to forget, let's work to remember. Grab a pen and your journal or a piece of paper. Prayerfully read the following statements. Write them in your journal, leaving space below each one to write. Ask God impact on you with the truth of each statement. Write whatever He brings to mind about each truth.

- I am a sinner. My sin, even if considered small to the world, is grievously heinous to the holy God who made me in His image.
- I was spiritually dead in sin with no hope of saving myself.
- While I was dead in my sin, God showed His love to me.
- Jesus gave His life and shed His blood to pay the debt my sin deserved.

- God forgave my sin, redeemed my life, and gave me a brand-new life in Christ.
- My salvation cost me nothing, but it cost God His Son.
- God brought me into a love relationship with Himself through Jesus.
- I will spend eternity in His presence, and even now He longs to fill my life with peace, joy, and purpose. And yes, passionate love for Him!

Did you seriously consider each truth? If we want to foster and maintain a passionate love for Jesus, we will never forget the miraculous work He has accomplished on our behalf. We will never forget that we are ugly sinners saved by God's beautiful grace. Don't let too much time pass before you remember again why you love Jesus.

Jesus knows our memories are short. That's one reason He instituted the Lord's Supper. Jesus established the cup and the bread to remind us of His shed blood and broken body. Each time we partake He wants us to purposefully remember Him and what He accomplished for us on the Cross (1 Corinthians 11:23–26). The next time you drink the cup and eat the bread, ask God to increase your love for Jesus. Ask Him to make you passionately crazy about your Savior.

Chapter 6

BEST-LAID PLANS

Attitude #4: Living for His Purposes

I've always been a planner. I need to know who, what, and when for every event, meal, and vacation for the rest of the decade. I have trouble with "last-minute" and "spontaneous." I'm thrown a bit off-balance when something does not come together just like I envisioned. When I was a little girl even my Barbie doll kept her calendar filled and up-to-date. This little personality quirk drives my husband crazy.

Although I know God wants me to stay organized and keep track of my commitments, He has also shown me that I need to hold my own plans more loosely. I can make my plans, but it is God's plan and purpose that will prevail (Proverbs 19:9). God is sovereign over my life and all of history. He has an end in mind and has chosen a way to accomplish that end. God has taught me that my planning and my purposes will not thwart His.

I've also learned that nothing and no one is here by chance. Many people wander aimlessly through life asking that age-old question, "Why am I here?" With no direction or sense of purpose, to them life feels meaningless and random. But God's Word clearly teaches just the opposite. God has a specific plan for this world, for humanity, for my life, and for your life. Each of us is here by God's design for a specific purpose and to do specific works. When we recognize that truth and find our place in God's plan, then our lives will be marked with significance and relevance. As we learn to walk in His way instead of our own way, our life of faith will be transformed from meaningless to fulfilling, dull to exciting!

The Big Picture

One weekend when our grown kids were visiting, we pulled out the old family videos. One scene in particular had us all laughing. Our second daughter, Sarah, was about two. My mother, the videographer, had the camera focused on her as she sat at the coffee table "coloring." Mom periodically asked Sarah questions in an attempt to capture her baby talk on film. Apparently our older daughter Kelley—then about four years old—could not stand the fact that she was not the subject of the video. The entire time the camera was running Kelley was running circles around Mom. Every few seconds, Kelley—with her blonde curls bouncing—would pass between Sarah and the camera. While she ran she counted. "1 . . . 2 . . . 3 . . . 4 . . . 5 . . . 6 . . ." Not only did Kelley want to be on camera, she also wanted the audience to know she was smart. Obviously, she thought the camera should be on her.

This little family story perfectly demonstrates our own human nature. Each and every one of us tends to think we are the center of the universe. Intellectually, we admit that God is supreme. We agree with the author of Hebrews that everything exists by God and for God (Hebrews 2:10). But the way we live doesn't always match what we say we believe. We make plans and then ask God to bless them. We decide how we want to serve God and assume He will be pleased. We calendar and budget and then see what time and money we have left for God and other people.

The Bible says God created humanity for His glory (Isaiah 43:7). God formed and made us to bring Him praise and honor. That is the primary purpose of every man, woman, and child — to glorify God. Even the heavens were made for His glory. *The heavens tell of the glory of God. The skies display his marvelous craftsmanship. Day after day they continue to speak; night after night they make him known* (Psalm 19:1–2 NLT). God is the Center of the universe and the purpose of our existence is to glorify Him.

God not only created us for His glory, He also *re-created* us for His glory. *"In him we were also chosen, having been predestined according to the plan of him who works out everything in conformity with the purpose of his will, in order that we, who were the first to put our hope in Christ, might be for the praise of his glory"* (Ephesians 1:11–12). God forgave our sins and gave us eternal life in Christ so we would praise Him! He purchased our redemption and guaranteed our eternal inheritance with the presence of His Spirit so we would have more cause to give Him glory. *The Spirit is God's guarantee that he will give us everything he promised and that he has purchased us to be his own people. This is just one more reason for us to praise our glorious God* (Ephesians 1:14 NLT).

This big picture purpose for all humanity — to glorify God — is also the highest purpose in life for each of us as individuals. God made me to bring Him glory. God made you to bring Him glory. The Apostle Paul understood this and took this truth to its logical conclusion: *"So, whether you eat or drink, or whatever you do, do all to the glory of God"* (1 Corinthians 10:31 ESV). Although Paul wrote this statement in the context of helping the Corinthian Christians decide whether or not to eat meat that had been sacrificed to idols, the truth principle applies across the board. Every decision we make and every action we take should be done with the purpose of bringing glory to God. "Will God be honored if I act in *this* way?" "Will other people praise God if I do *this*?"

The whole of creation, life in general, humanity at large, and even each of us individually all exist to bring glory to God. He is the Center of the universe. He is to be the Center of *my* universe. He is to be the Center of *your* universe. My life is not about me. That's something I need to remind myself of every day.

A Greater Purpose

When we first consider the truth that our lives are not about us, we may feel a bit disappointed. We had big plans and dreams. We had much to do for ourselves and so much to accomplish for God. But that is faulty thinking. Our vision is too narrow. We fail to see God's big picture. He has an ultimate purpose, a big, overarching plan that He is working out in time.

God orchestrates His overall purposes and plans through the annals of history. He makes nations great and destroys them as He determines (Job 12:23). He raises kingdoms up and tears them down according to His will. He decides who will lead them and where they will be located on the planet (Acts 17:26). Before He ever created the world, God had a plan for the end of time. And His plan will not be thwarted.

> *And do not forget the things I have done throughout history. For I am God—I alone! I am God, and there is no one else like me. Only I can tell you what is going to happen even before it happens. Everything I plan will come to pass, for I do whatever I wish (Isaiah 46:9–10 NLT).*

God's purpose in all this is for people to seek Him and find Him (Acts 17:24–28). He is constantly working to move everything toward Himself. Over and over, Scripture tells us that at the end of earthly time, all people will stand before God, bow their knee to Him, and confess "Jesus Christ is Lord, to the glory of God the Father" (Philippians 2:11; Romans 14:11; Isaiah 45:23). Every person *will* confess Jesus Christ as Lord—that is God's will and it will happen. The question all of us must answer for ourselves is whether we will submit to God now or on Judgment Day. If we bend the knee to God now, we can bring Him glory in this life through a loving, joyful, and fulfilling relationship with Jesus (John 10:10). And we also get to spend eternity with Him. If we reject Christ now, we will still bend our knee at the end of time, but we will be separated from God for all eternity.

God wants you to be a part of His plan for humanity. You are a significant player in God's big scheme. But it's still His plan and His way. Henry Blackaby and Claude King teach this truth in their highly recognized book and study *Experiencing God.* "He (God) has a purpose and plan for your life. But the plan He has for your life is based on what He is doing in His world. He has a great purpose in mind for all humankind throughout all time. His desire is for you to become involved in what He is doing."[1] God wants to involve you in His overall plan to turn hearts to Jesus. The sovereign God, the one true Creator wants to involve us in His plans. Yes, we can plan doable-sized plans and dream human-sized dreams, but they are so puny in light of God's purposes. Wouldn't you rather step into His purposes for your life? Remember, He is "able to do far more abundantly than all that we ask or think" (Ephesians 3:20). I certainly don't want to settle for something I can think up.

You Have a Part in His Plan

I want to be a part of God's plan to turn hearts to Jesus! How about you? If your answer is yes, you may be wondering what that should look like in your everyday life. God's primary, overall purpose for everyone is the same: to bring Him glory through an obedient and loving relationship with Jesus. But, the specific, day-to-day workings of that will look different for each of us. God has a specific plan, a unique set of works and service for me and for you. My part in His big picture plan is different than yours.

Scripture repeatedly illustrates the spiritual truth that God has specific works and a distinct plan for different people. For instance, God planned for Jeremiah to be a prophet to the nations before he was formed in his mother's womb (Jeremiah 1:5). Not only did God give Jeremiah a particular job, He also gave him the specific assignments and the exact words to say (1:7–10). It did not take long for Jeremiah to learn that God had the right to determine what his life should look like (10:23).

Peter learned from Jesus that he would die a certain kind of death for the purpose of bringing glory to God (John 21:18–19). The Apostle Paul recognized that God had given him a special ministry of taking the good news of Jesus to the Gentiles (Ephesians 3:1–2). Job knew that God has the authority to determine the number of our days and set limits for our lives (Job 14:5). David understood that even before God began to knit his body together He had already determined each of his days (Psalm 139:16). Queen Esther discovered that God placed her in a particular relationship at a particular time in history to accomplish a particular task — to save His people from an evil madman's scheme of annihilation. God had a unique plan for Esther for "just such a time as this" (Esther 4:14 NLT).

So Jeremiah, Peter, Paul, Job, David, and Esther knew God had a unique plan for their lives. But does God have a unique plan for each and every one of us? And if He does, then how do we discover what God's plans are for us in the here and now? What is our "just such a time as this"?

Scripture makes it clear that God saved us by His grace through faith in Jesus Christ and not by anything we have done (Ephesians 2:8–9). However, Scripture makes it just as clear that God saved us *for* good works. He had a specific purpose in our salvation. He determined particular tasks and acts of service for each of us before He saved us (Ephesians 2:10). Some of you may be furiously flipping back through chapter 3. "Didn't she say that faith is about Who we know and not what we do?" Yes, our faith is defined by our relationship with Jesus. But as we relate to Him in love and obedience, the works He has planned for us should be a natural outflow of the relationship (John 15:5). The key is to say yes to the tasks, ministries, and acts of service that God planned in advance for us to do and no to those things He has planned for someone else.

Uniquely Equipped for a Unique Purpose

How do you discover God's specific will for you? Start by examining how He has equipped you. *Wait, before we go any further, I need to interject a word of clarification and caution.* Remember the plan is God's plan. Out of His love for us, He allows us to participate in His plan. One of the primary principles in Scripture—and beautifully taught in *Experiencing God*—is that God is always at work around us and invites us to join Him in His work. We would be guilty of making it about us if we merely looked at ourselves with the purpose of determining what we should do for God. However, it is also clear from Scripture that God has equipped each of us for His service. So, while focusing on God and His plan, let's move forward with humility.

God has outfitted you with a unique set of spiritual gifts, talents, resources, training, and life experiences. No one else has just that combination. God gave *you* what *you* need to carry out

His specific purposes for you. In his best-selling book *The Purpose Driven Life*, author and Pastor Rick Warren refers to this unique equipping as our "shape." Warren uses SHAPE as an acronym for the spiritual gifts, heart, abilities, personality, and experience God has given each of us.[2] Here's a bit of what Warren says about our unique "shape."

> Only you can be you. God designed each of us so there would be no duplication in the world. No one has the exact same mix of factors that make you unique. That means no one else on earth will ever be able to play the role God planned for you. If you don't make your unique contribution to the body of Christ, it won't be made.[3]

Yes, God has specific work for you to do. But God also specifically prepared you to complete it. You are uniquely significant for His plans and purposes.

Gifts of the Holy Spirit usually come to mind first when we consider our equipping for God's service. Paul gives a lot of relevant facts about spiritual gifts in the 12th chapter of 1 Corinthians (1 Corinthians 12:4–11). The Holy Spirit is the source of all spiritual gifts. He alone determines how they should be distributed. Our gifting is up to Him, not us. The same Spirit indwells each Christian but manifests Himself differently in each of our lives through the gifts He gives us. His plan is for us to bring Him glory by using these gifts in service and ministry to help the church (1 Peter 4:10–11). But your spiritual gifting is only part of the way God has uniquely equipped you for His service.

Nothing has come into your life by chance. Our sovereign God ordained each of your days before they came to pass. God uses every relationship, educational opportunity, and circumstance to mold you into His servant. He also gave you talents and passions to shape you for His service. God wants you to use your unique equipping to participate in His work. He wants the person with your specific combination of gifts, talents, and experiences to fill a role in His plan.

A Personal Example

In the first chapter I shared how God used a women's Bible study to fan the fires of my faith. God used that experience to foster within me a passion for His Word and for women's Bible study. As the years passed, He gave me opportunities to teach numerous small groups, train other teachers, and even coordinate all the women's study groups in one church. As I obeyed Him in each step, He continued to give me opportunities to participate in His plan.

One particular year, as the time to begin the women's fall Bible studies drew close, I received a call from Margy, the church secretary. Two separate women from the community, who had brought their children to our Vacation Bible School, had called the church that morning to ask if we offered a Bible study class for women who had never studied the Bible before. Since that was my area of responsibility, Margy called me. I knew immediately that God was working in these women's hearts.

I had already chosen the studies that would be offered and recruited the women to lead them. The books were ordered. The flyers were copied. (Remember, I'm a planner.) But even this type A girl knew God was up to something exciting and I wanted to be a part of it. I told Margy that I would make sure it happened and asked her to call the women and let them know. I found material and juggled the other classes and teachers.

Four women attended the study. Two of them accepted Jesus as their Savior before the study ended. God continued to work in the lives of the other two and within a few months they too became Christians. That small group was just the beginning of what God wanted to do. He continued to bring adults to our church who knew nothing about the Bible. Sometimes they just showed up on Sunday morning. Sometimes they expressed interest in spiritual things to one of our members. But they kept coming.

We moved the Seeker class to Sunday mornings to accommodate the people God was sending our way. As soon as one ten-week session finished, there was another group waiting to get started. Through teaching several of these groups, I learned the students' most frequent questions, what they needed to learn from the Bible, and in what order they needed it to be taught. The material we were using did not meet that need. By that time God had uniquely equipped me to write the curriculum that would meet that need.

God began working in the hearts of two moms. He had equipped and prepared me to take part in His plan. I had the great thrill and blessing of personally seeing dozens of people come to know Jesus as their Savior through the subsequent small groups. But God did not stop there. That curriculum He equipped me to write is now *God's Truth Revealed,* a 12-session Bible study on the foundations of the Christian faith. It has been used by individuals and churches across North America and around the world to discover what it means to know Jesus. God started it all with two phone calls to a church secretary, and He allowed me to tag along. That certainly fired up my faith.

Your Turn

I did not know everything *God* had planned when I changed *my* plans for women's Bible study. But He had prepared and equipped me to be a part His activity. I simply took that first step of obedience. You will probably not see all God has planned when He invites you to take part in something He is doing. But you will miss out on the joy and excitement of taking part in His plan if you don't take that first step.

Your first step of obedience will look different from mine. God has equipped you differently than He has equipped me. He has a unique part in His big picture plan just for you. God does not ask every Christian to teach the Bible to spiritual seekers. Perhaps He has equipped you to teach preschoolers. Maybe He has prepared you to stock and maintain a food pantry at your church. Or maybe your life experiences have uniquely shaped you to be a listening ear and the shoulder someone cries on. I don't know the specific role God has equipped you for. But I do know He has equipped you to take part in His plan. Scripture clearly teaches that God calls *every* Christian to glorify Him through loving, serving, building up, sharing, and growing. He has a place of ministry for you. How can you make sure you don't miss out?

First, watch for how God is working in the lives and circumstances around you. In *Experiencing God,* Blackaby and King identify from Scripture activities that only God can accomplish. Again, only God can draw people to Jesus (John 6:44); only God can give people understanding of spiritual things (1 Corinthians 2:12–14); and only God can convict people of sin (John 16:8).[4] If you witness any of these things, you can be sure that God is working.

Next, ask Him for guidance on how you can take part in His plans. How has He uniquely equipped you to play a role in this particular instance? When Margy called me, I immediately knew God was working. I also knew exactly how God had prepared me to take part in His plans. I could "reorganize" and I could teach. So I did. And I was tremendously blessed.

Take a few moments to consider prayerfully how God is currently working around you. Are there specific people who are seeking Jesus, asking spiritual questions, or struggling to live holy lives? Is there a specific circumstance where God is obviously at work? Jot those people and circumstances in your journal or the margin of this book. Now ask God to show you how He has uniquely equipped you to participate in His plans.

Don't be discouraged if He doesn't shout it out to you right now. Finding your place in His plans is a process. And often it is one small step of obedience at a time. Then occasionally, He will allow you to see a bigger picture of what He's done. Keep watching. Continue to pray. Then when you see Him working His plan around you, jump in!

Chapter 7

FROM HERE TO ETERNITY

Attitude #5: Eternal Perspective

Helen Roseveare spent almost two decades dispensing medical care and eternal hope in the rainforests of Africa. In 1953, Dr. Roseveare left the material comforts of Great Britain for the Belgian Congo to serve as a medical missionary. For the first 12 years she built village hospitals, treated every illness and injury, loved the people, and told them about Jesus. Then in 1964, her circumstances turned from physically difficult to excruciating.

Political unrest marked the Congo in the early 1960s. Although danger and instability were rampant, Dr. Roseveare chose to stay and continue her work. In 1964, violence escalated with the onset of a civil war. Dozens of missionaries were slaughtered and 200 Catholic priests and nuns were murdered. One Saturday afternoon in August, rebel forces entered Roseveare's village. Some of them invaded her home. That night Roseveare was brutally beaten and raped. The rebels took her and a small group of other missionaries captive. For five long months she endured continued violence at the hands of her captors.

After her rescue in January 1965, Dr. Roseveare returned to England, but only stayed about a year. In 1966, she went back to the Congo. Much work remained to be done. The doctor spent the next seven years rebuilding hospitals, establishing a medical school, and training doctors and nurses to care for the Congolese people in the name of Jesus. Why did she return? It certainly would have been safer back in England. After all that hardship and suffering I probably would have stayed to enjoy the comforts and security of home.

Now or Forever?

Dr. Roseveare's eternal perspective propelled her back to the Congo. She could not remain in the United Kingdom when people in Africa had "never yet heard of our Lord Jesus Christ and of the redemption He wrought for them at Calvary."[1] Even after her return to the west in 1973, she spoke and wrote to inspire other Christians to live in a way that reflected their certain hope in Christ's return. Our costly redemption and the ongoing transformative work wrought in us by the Holy Spirit were more than enough incentive for Roseveare. In her book *Living Holiness,* she encourages readers to live holy lives, secure in Christ's return, with a "longing in our hearts to be found watching and waiting to welcome Him."[2]

I must admit, when I read about Christians like Helen Roseveare, I feel like a hypocrite. Although I believe and teach we must live our lives focused on the eternal, I still sometimes find myself living for the temporary. I still favor my comfort, my time, and my things too much. The temporary still has too much influence on my decisions and actions. I still often moan, "Why me?" when trials and difficulties hit. And I still sometimes hesitate to talk about Jesus for fear of how someone else may react.

Many Christians get stuck in the demands of the here and now. Temporal activities pull us away from eternal matters. We pour our time and energy into the "delights" of this world and end up with little of lasting value. We often choose physical comfort over spiritual growth and refinement. But gaining the comforts of this world satisfies us only temporarily. Earthly pleasures all wear out and lose their appeal. And when the difficulties of life come we are thrown off balance. Living for today leaves our faith dry because we've gained nothing that lasts.

I believe Christians in America have a particularly hard time living for eternity. The religious freedom we enjoy and our country's relatively high standard of living make it easy to practice our faith with a "here and now" perspective. Very little in our culture challenges us to choose between Jesus and the comforts of our daily lives. In fact, on the surface they seem to blend quite nicely.

In his book *Radical,* author David Platt describes how the American church has been shaped by our culture more than the American culture has been shaped by the church. "We Christians are living out the American dream in the context of our communities of faith."[3] Platt says the answer to taking our faith back from the American dream is to develop an eternal perspective.

> The key is realizing — and believing — that this world is not your home. If you and I ever hope to free our lives from worldly desires, worldly thinking, worldly pleasures, worldly dreams, worldly ideas, worldly values, worldly ambitions, and worldly acclaim, then we must focus our lives on another world. Though you and I live in the United States of America now, we must fix our attention on a "better country — a heavenly one" (Luke 14:33).[4]

God created us for eternity; His purposes are eternal. The things of God have lasting value. Learning to live with eternity in mind will help us keep life's trials in perspective, welcome God's refinement, and teach us to depend on Him. When we invest our time, energy, and resources in the eternal, our faith will be ignited with the assurance that we are storing our "treasures in heaven, where neither moth or rust destroys and where thieves do not break in and steal" (Matthew 6:20 ESV).

How do we know if our faith is influenced more by the temporal or the eternal? In this chapter we will consider two areas particularly prone to temporal influence. By examining the way we respond to our trials and how we invest our resources, we can better determine if we are living for eternity or the here and now.

Light and Momentary

About ten years ago my spiritual growth hit a plateau. I did not feel as though my faith was in decline, but I knew I was not growing. My relationship with Christ was not deepening. However, several of my friends were growing rapidly in their faith. I noticed that all of them were facing severe trials — things like serious illness or the loss of a loved one. These difficulties sent them running straight to Jesus. As they clung to Him in dependence their faith blossomed.

In contrast, my life was relatively easy. Without any major problems, stresses, or dilemmas, I was handling things just fine. So why was my faith stagnant? Life was *too* easy. My friends learned to lean on God out of necessity. I thought I could stand on my own. Then God reminded me of the many Scripture passages that teach how God uses the trials of this life to refine our faith and grow us into the likeness of Christ.

The Apostle Paul taught the Roman Christians to rejoice in their problems and trials, knowing that "they are good for us — they help us endure. And endurance develops strength of character in us, and character strengthens our confident expectation of salvation" (Romans 5:3–4 NLT). The Lord's brother James wrote,

"Whenever trouble comes your way, let it be an opportunity for joy. For when your faith is tested, your endurance has a chance to grow. So let it grow, for when your endurance is fully developed, you will be strong in character and ready for anything" (James 1:2–4 NLT).

The Apostle Peter penned my favorite passage about the purpose of our trials.

So be truly glad! There is wonderful joy ahead, even though it is necessary for you to endure many trials for a while. These trials are only to test your faith, to show that it is strong and pure. It is being tested as fire tests and purifies gold — and your faith is far more precious to God than mere gold. So if your faith remains strong after being tried by fiery trials, it will bring you much praise and glory and honor on the day when Jesus Christ is revealed to the whole world (1 Peter 1:6–7 NLT).

I realized I needed a little difficulty. Believe it or not, I began to pray that God would refine my faith. And yes, I knew what that would require. And yes, God answered my prayers in the affirmative. Soon refining trials filled my life. A rebellious teenage daughter, the loss of a family member in a tragic car accident, and a 2,000-mile move across country were just the beginning.

I am not saying that God caused my daughter's rebellion or my mother-in-law's death to answer my prayer for refinement. I know that God is completely sovereign. But the way His sovereignty works in the sinful and painful things of this life is far beyond the scope of this chapter and the wisdom of this author. However, the following biblical truths will help us view our trials from God's perspective:

- Our all-powerful God controls every situation (Psalm 77:14; Jeremiah 32:17; Ephesians 1:18–21).
- God knows and cares about every detail of our lives (Matthew 6:25–34; Hebrews 4:15; Philippians 4:19).
- God is good, loving, and faithful (Psalm 145:17; 1 John 4:8; Lamentations 3:22–23).
- God is always with us in the midst of our trials (Isaiah 43:2; Psalm 23:4; John 14:16; Matthew 28:20).
- God strengthens and comforts His children in the midst of our troubles (Psalm 147:3; Isaiah 40:27–13; 2 Corinthians 1:3–4; Philippians 4:13).
- God works through difficulties in our lives to accomplish His eternal purposes (James 1:2–4; Romans 5:3–5; 1 Peter 1:6–7; Romans 8:28–29).

While God cares deeply about our physical circumstances, He is even more concerned about our spiritual condition. God wants all His children to resemble His Son Jesus. He is constantly working in our lives to transform us into the image of Christ (Romans 8:29). God uses the "light and momentary troubles" of this life to bring about His eternal purposes for us. The Apostle Paul reminded the Corinthian Christians of this same truth:

> *Therefore we do not lose heart. Though outwardly we are wasting away, yet inwardly we are being renewed day by day. For our light and momentary troubles are achieving for us an eternal glory that far outweighs*

them all. So we fix our eyes not on what is seen, but on what is unseen, since what is seen is temporary, but what is unseen is eternal. (2 Corinthians 4:16–18).

Paul faced enough hardship and heartache for several lifetimes, yet he recognized God used them all for His purposes. God worked in Paul's trials to refine his faith, spread the gospel to new areas, and bring others into a saving relationship with Jesus. God brought glory to Himself through Paul's momentary suffering. Paul could be joyful in the middle of the hard times because he learned to focus on the eternal rather than his temporary circumstances.

How have you responded to trials in the past? Have you been able to focus on the eternal or have you been overwhelmed by the temporary? If we fix our eyes on Jesus during times of difficulty, God will strengthen us in our weakness, guide us through to the other side, and use the hardship to draw us closer to Him. Unfortunately, sometimes we lose site of the eternal and allow the temporary to overwhelm us. Instead of faithfully clinging to God when trials hit, we respond with doubt, anger, or even rebellion. We can end up even farther away from God.

This particular time, when difficulties escalated in my own life, I knew God wanted to use them to strengthen and grow my stagnant faith. I did not want to waste the tears, grief, and pain. God taught me to lean on Him in the midst of trials and watch for how He works out His eternal purposes through my temporal circumstances. I can't say that this is always my first reaction when hard times hit, but each time it gets easier to "refocus" on eternity.

In *Radical,* Platt says God

"intentionally puts his people in situations where they come face to face with their need for him. In the process, he powerfully demonstrates his ability to provide everything his people need in ways they could have never mustered up or imagined. And in the end, he makes much of his own name."[5]

Now when trials come, even though I do not welcome the struggle itself, I do anticipate what God will do through it.

Each time trials come we have a choice to make. Will we focus on Christ with an eternal perspective and choose to trust Him to accomplish His purposes? Or will we doubt God will do what He promises and allow the temporary to overwhelm us?

Worth the Investment

God not only wants eternity to impact the way we view our trials, He also wants His eternal purposes to affect how we invest our resources. As God faithfully works to shape us into the image of Christ, eternal things will influence us more and more. Increasingly we will want to use what God has given us to build His kingdom rather than ours.

In the last chapter, we explored the biblical truth that God has uniquely equipped each of us to fill a specific role in His big picture plan. God has designed every element, brought together every piece of your life, to prepare you to serve Him. His equipping includes your talents, spiritual gifts, life experiences, education, and training. His design for service also includes the resources He has blessed you with—your time, physical energy, finances, intellect, creativity, and more.

So many things compete for our resources. We are constantly bombarded with demands and requests from others, particularly for our time and finances. And our own desires and interests draw on them as well. The problem is that all of our resources are limited. We have just so much time, strength, and money. Will we choose to invest them in the temporary or the eternal? In things that last or soon disappear?

In recent years our country's economy has suffered one downturn after another. Many people have lost their homes, jobs, or life's savings. Even "safe" investments are not necessarily safe. This devastating situation in our nation reinforces the truth that temporary things are just that—temporary. Our money, health, and material possessions can be gone in an instant. Yet we continue to yield to the temptation to invest in the temporary over the eternal.

In the Sermon on the Mount, Jesus emphasized the need to devote our resources to things that last.

> *"Don't store up treasures here on earth, where moths eat them and rust destroys them, and where thieves break in and steal. Store your treasures in heaven, where moths and rust cannot destroy, and thieves do not break in and steal. Wherever your treasure is, there the desires of your heart will also be" (Matthew 6:19–21 NLT).*

Everything valuable in the eyes of the world will one day be worthless. The photos and memories of that once-in-a-lifetime vacation quickly fade. The value of that new car drops drastically the day you drive it off the lot. All the time you spend at work can be undone with one small slip of pink paper. But the things of God will never lose their value. In fact, when we invest in eternal things God takes our puny offerings and multiplies them many times over. The joy and excitement of participating in God's eternal purposes cannot be duplicated.

The way we choose to spend our money, use our time, and expend our energy should reflect God's purposes. This does not mean we should never take fun trips, buy something simply because we like it, or spend two hours at the movies with the family. It does mean that every choice we make should first be filtered through the light of eternity. God's eternal purposes take priority. If a choice must be made between using a resource to build God's kingdom and using a resource for something temporary, the eternal things of God should come first.

One particular frustration continues to stand out to me as an example of allowing the temporary to take priority over the eternal. For several years in a row, God placed me in the role of Vacation Bible School director for our church. VBS is often the biggest outreach effort of the year for a local church, with the potential to reach many unchurched families with the news about Jesus.

The most difficult thing about this tough job is recruiting the workers needed to make it happen. I always started publicizing the date and the positions needed early in the year. I wanted to get the information out *before* the church members made their summer plans. But every year I was discouraged and shocked to get the same response from dozens of potential workers. "I can't tell you right now whether or not I can help. We haven't decided on our summer plans yet. Once we get our vacation scheduled I'll let you know if I'm available."

Maybe you've heard—or even said—something like this in a similar situation. My goal is not to point fingers. I've put temporary things over the eternal more times than I even realize. But this common occurrence illustrates how a temporal perspective affects many Christians. These Christians were willing to serve. They even felt like God would have them serve in VBS. But they would commit to serve only if the date did not conflict with their personal calendar—a calendar over which they had control. A Christian with a solid eternal perspective would put Vacation Bible School—or another missional activity such as this—on the calendar first, then plan their other summer activities around it.

How can we foster an eternal perspective about the use of our resources? First, we need to remember who gave them to us. In his first letter, the Apostle Peter encourages Christians to remember we are merely stewards of everything God has given us.

> *As each has received a gift, use it to serve one another, as good stewards of God's varied grace: whoever speaks, as one who speaks oracles of God; whoever serves, as one who serves by the strength that God supplies — in order that in everything God may be glorified through Jesus Christ. To him belong glory and dominion forever and ever. Amen* (1 Peter 4:10–11 ESV).

We readily recognize that God is the source of our talents and spiritual gifts. However, we often forget that *every* "good and perfect gift" comes from our heavenly Father (James 1:17). He created time. He formed our bodies. He gives us the strength to work and play. He even gives us money so we can be generous with His gift and use it in His service (2 Corinthians 9:11–12).

A second way we can foster an eternal perspective in using our resources is through periodic self-evaluation. When we look at how and where we spend our time, money, energy, and other resources, we may be shocked at how little of it we invest in things that last. For instance, compare your number of family trips and vacations to time and money spent on missions endeavors. Time and energy spent preparing to teach a Bible lesson versus time spent watching television or playing fantasy football.

I am not against vacations, television, or even fantasy football. I enjoy spending time on many of these things — fantasy football excluded. However, so often we consume most of our resources with things that don't last and give God the leftovers. God gave us all these good things and made us stewards over their use. He asks us to use our first and best for His purposes. Will we use them for the here and now or for eternity?

Fired Up for Eternity

I am still working to live with a consistent eternal perspective. Trials of this life sometimes still overwhelm me. Occasionally I still waste time, money, or energy on things that won't last until tomorrow. Periodically, I still pass up investing in the eternal in favor of the temporary. But God continues to show me that living for the things of this life will leave me empty. Excitement over worldly things is awesome — for about 20 minutes. Then life moves on and we start looking for something new.

Three thousand years ago, wise King Solomon came to the same conclusion about living with a temporal perspective. Solomon had the money, power, and authority to acquire anything and everything he wanted. He denied himself no earthly pleasure or vice. He planned, built, and accomplished all he set his mind to. Yet when he considered it all, he declared it to be empty. "Everything is meaningless," says the Teacher, "utterly meaningless! No matter how much we see, we are never satisfied. No matter how much we hear, we are not content" (Ecclesiastes 1:2, 8 NLT).

No amount of worldly success, acclaim, or stuff will last any longer than my last breath. In the scope of eternity, it is all meaningless. But the things of God — the things that impact souls for Christ — will never rot, crumble, or fade away. We must look beyond the things of this world to find true meaning and relevance for life. God programmed us for eternity. He wired us to find fulfillment and excitement in the things that last beyond the physical. Living with an eternal perspective can generate an excitement and passion your faith has been missing. Don't wait any longer. Ask God now to help you live life for all eternity.

PART THREE:

READY, SET, ACTION!

Chapter 8

FEAST ON THE WORD

Action #1: Diligently Read and Study the Bible

The people on the street crowded in tight around us. They stretched out their arms desperately wanting to snag a copy for themselves. In just a few hectic days, our short-term missions team gave away 10,000 Bibles to the spiritually hungry citizens of Moscow. That was September 1991, roughly two weeks after an attempted coup. Bible distribution in the Soviet Union had been limited and closely monitored for nearly a century. Only a relative few enjoyed the privilege of owning a Bible. Many more hungered for God's Word.

Do you long for God's Word like that? If you didn't have a Bible, would you stand in a line for hours to own one? Later in this chapter we will discuss five specific ways to develop an insatiable appetite for Scripture. God Himself will foster this hunger if you step out in obedience to pursue it.

Are You Hungry?

Whether we acknowledge the source of our hunger or not, we humans long to connect with our Creator, to intimately know the God of the universe. God satisfies this spiritual hunger of our souls through His inspired Word. He reveals Himself, His character, and His ways in the Bible. In his autobiography, George Müller called the Bible "food for the inner man."

Life-threatening problems result when our physical bodies don't get enough healthy food. Weakness from loss of muscle mass, anemia, and difficulty concentrating are just the beginning. Vital organs also begin to shrink and lose the ability to function. Our physical bodies cannot live for long without nutritious food. Likewise, our souls will lack health and vitality without a spiritual diet rich in God's Word.

George Müller believed a Christian's primary source of spiritual nourishment is the Word of God. Many of today's Christian leaders agree:

- "The soul is awakened to God chiefly by the Spirit of God as he pierces our souls with the Word of God."[1]
- "The primary means of growth God has given us is His Word."[2]
- "The Bible is no empty word, but it is your very life—the kindling of your joy!"[3]

Experience confirms this in my life. Not long after I confessed my struggle with flat faith during my "turning point" conversation with my "fiery-faithed" friend Susan, I joined that Bible study through the Book of Romans. Until then, my relationship with God's Word had been far too casual. I had been *reading* the Bible my whole life, but I had never *absorbed* it before. Finally, the combination of my vulnerable, "desperate for God" attitude and a *serious* approach to God's Word proved to be rich fare for my hungry soul.

As I approached the Bible with this new desperation, the Spirit of God illuminated truths I had read before, yet had never internalized. As I continued to study, excitement over what God was teaching me blossomed into passion for His Word. This passion kept driving me back to the Bible. Now, almost three decades later, my love affair with the Bible is still going strong. In his book, *The Soul's*

Quest for God, R. C. Sproul writes about this difference between having God's Word in our minds and in our hearts.

> "When the Word of God gets beyond the mind and into the heart, then and only then do our lives really change. We pass from a consciousness of the Word of God to a conviction of it, and then to a conscience that delights in it."[4]

Even if we come with the right attitude, casual approaches to the Bible will seldom foster passion or usher us into God's presence. We must go beyond cursory daily readings and study that merely increases knowledge. Later in this chapter, we will delve into several practical disciplines to deepen our desire for feasting on God's Word and the benefits we can derive. First, however, let's consider the disconnect that exists for many Christians between what we believe about the Bible and our practice.

Feast or Famine?

The Bible holds the distinction of being not only the first book ever to be printed but also the best-selling book of all time. In fact, the Bible continues to be the top seller of the year — year after year — with about 25 million copies sold annually in the United States alone. According to a 2006 *New Yorker* article by Daniel Radosh, research shows that 91 percent of American households own at least one Bible and the average household owns four. Reflecting on these statistics, Radosh wrote, "Bible publishers manage to sell 25 million copies a year of a book that almost everybody already has."[5]

I just took an inventory of all the Bibles in our house. The result? Twenty-one Bibles in nine different translations. That inventory does not include the Bibles in my office at church. Or the numerous translations I can read online. Or on my phone. Abundant audio versions allow us to listen to the Bible in our cars, at the gym, or anywhere else we can take our various handheld devices. Access to God's Word today has never been greater or more varied.

Unfortunately, the numbers of those who actually read the Bible regularly do not reflect the high level of ownership and accessibility. Pollster George Gallup Jr. has been widely quoted as saying, "Americans revere the Bible, but, by and large, they don't read it." Polls show that only about a third of American Christians read the Bible on their own one or more times each week.[6] How physically healthy would we be if we ate less than once a week?

The majority of evangelical Christians believe what the Bible teaches about itself:

- It is the very words of God; physically recorded by the hands of men as inspired by the Spirit of God. God breathed out His Word through humans for humans (2 Timothy 3:16).
- God's Word is alive and active in our lives and the lives of those around us. It is not static or bound by time. It crosses all cultural barriers, language differences, and geographical borders (Hebrews 4:12).
- The Holy Spirit wields God's Word like a sword to pierce our hearts and reveal our sinful thoughts, attitudes, and motivations (Hebrews 4:12–13).
- He lays it out beside our lives as a measuring rod to teach, correct, and equip us in preparation for God's purposes (2 Timothy 3:16–17).

God longs to lovingly apply His Word like a balm to our souls, to heal our hurts, comfort our grief, and fill us with His joy. Yet often we fail to give Him the opportunity. If we really believe that the Bible is the very words of God to us and for us, then why don't we read it? Why do we fail to taste its sweetness? We've allowed our fast-food, high-speed Internet culture to shape even the way we approach the Bible. I confess, I still sometimes allow the busyness of life to pressure me to get "in and out" of the Bible and on to my full day ahead. Yet to be truly affected by God's Word, to be transformed by the Holy Scriptures, we must slow down. Linger over it. Savor every word. We cannot experience its earth-shaking power on the run.

Ezra, one of my favorite biblical heroes, not only knew God's Word has power, he also experienced it. A priest and teacher of God's law, Ezra was a Jewish exile serving under the Persian king Artaxerxes during the fifth century B.C. The Bible records that he was "well versed" in the Law of Moses (Ezra 7:6). Ezra didn't know just enough of God's Word "to get by." He was *skilled* in it. The original language shows that Ezra was equipped and prepared for any task to which God called him.

We also learn that Ezra had "devoted himself to the study and observance of the Law of the LORD and to teaching its decrees and laws in Israel" (Ezra 7:10). Ezra had firmly committed in his heart and mind to learn God's Word. Reading, reflecting, and meditating on Scripture was an enduring, lifelong pursuit. Ezra's devoted study of God's Word was not merely for intellectual development. He also applied the things God taught him. Ezra obeyed God, thus submitting himself to God's transforming power.

Ezra's devotion to diligent study and obedience in turn birthed passion. This passion drove him all the way to Jerusalem to teach God's people the Law they'd forgotten. Ezra's deep love for God's Word shaped the purpose for his life. He embarked on a four-month, arduous journey from Babylon to Palestine in the heat of the summer. But God favored Ezra for his obedience. Twice, the Book of Ezra records that the "gracious hand of God was on him" (Ezra 7:6, 9).

I love that! I want that! Do you long for the gracious hand of God to rest on you? To touch your very soul with His blessing? Then devote yourself to the study and observance of His Word.

Food for the Soul

What benefits *do* we derive from spending time in God's Word? Obviously, reading and studying the Bible increases our knowledge. We learn about God, His character, and how He works among His people. Mere intellectual knowledge is just the beginning. It simply lays the foundation for the more important work God wants to do in us. Real feasting on the spiritual food God supplies also feeds our souls.

People who know me have said that when they read one of my books they can "hear" me; they can mentally picture me saying the words they're reading. The words on the page are more alive for these readers because we are friends. They know my personality and the tone of my voice. The friendship we share adds a unique dimension to their reading.

When Christians spend time in the Bible, we miss an incredible blessing if we merely read the words on the page. If we are Christians—followers of Christ—we know God. We have a personal relationship with the author of the Bible. The words of the Bible came directly from the heart of God as His Spirit worked through the minds and pens of men. We know the Author!

In *Desiring God,* John Piper writes about the incredible blessing we can receive from feasting on the Spirit-inspired Word. "The Spirit inspired the Word and therefore goes where the Word goes. The more of God's Word you know and love, the more of

God's Spirit you will experience."[7] When we truly ingest God's Word, we will taste the sweetness of the Author of Life. When we go beyond a superficial reading of the Bible, we will experience the Person of the Holy Spirit. We will interact with our Creator. That is the point when God will move our hearts and meet the deepest needs of our souls. The sense of His holiness will move us to worship. The awareness of His presence will fill us with His peace and comfort.

We've merely stuck our toes in the depths of blessings God will lavishly pour out on us when we indulge in the richness of His Word. The deeper we go below the surface, the more God's blessings will cover us. Here are a few more benefits in which to delight:

- Preparation for the future—God uses His Word to foster spiritual endurance and fill His children with hope and encouragement. Even if the days ahead are filled with trouble, pain, and persecution, we can be victorious every step of the way because God has prepared us through Scripture. *For everything that was written in the past was written to teach us, so that through endurance and the encouragement of the Scriptures we might have hope* (Romans 15:4).
- Strength to resist temptation—Jesus Himself used God's Word to stave off Satan's attacks. Scripture will protect us from sin by arming us with the truth and strengthening our longing to please and obey God. With God's Word in our hearts—not just in our minds—we can stand firm. *The law of his God is in his heart; his feet will not slip* (Psalm 37:31).
- Spiritual growth—God wants to grow us to be like Jesus. Ingesting Scripture fuels our spiritual growth. God actively uses His Word in our lives to shape our character, change our desires, and mold our motivations to the image of Christ. This spiritual

growth fosters a more intimate fellowship with Christ through a deeper knowledge of Him. *Like newborn babies, crave pure spiritual milk, so that by it you may grow up in your salvation, now that you have tasted that the Lord is good* (1 Peter 2:2–3).

- Spiritual vitality — Those who live a life rooted in Scripture will thrive. God will bless us when we delight in and are devoted to His Word. Our relationship with Him will be strong and produce eternal results. *He is like a tree planted by streams of water, which yields its fruit in season and whose leaf does not wither. Whatever he does prospers* (Psalm 1:3).

Again, this is only a sampling of the rich buffet of blessings God's Word can produce in our lives. However, we can't receive any benefits from God's spiritual food unless we partake. Let's discuss how we can foster our appetite for God's Word and consider some specific ways we can interact with Scripture to encounter the Author.

Create a Craving

My stomach is growling while I write these words. It's almost lunchtime, and my belly does not want me to forget that fact. However, remembering to eat has never been a problem for me. Often, as I finish one meal, I'm already planning the next one! Do you feel that way about God's Word? Does your heart draw you to partake regularly, or do you sometimes forget to fill your soul? Do you anxiously anticipate your next opportunity to sit down with your Bible, or does reading God's Word feel like a dry, mundane chore?

You can foster a growing desire for Scripture. The more you take in God's Word, the more you will experience its power. The more you experience its power, the more you will want to savor God's Word again and again. My love affair with chocolate helps me understand this phenomenon. The more I indulge in its dark, creamy sweetness, the more of it I want. But the opposite is also true. The more I deprive myself of enjoying this special treat, the less I think about it.

When we limit our intake of God's Word, our desire for it diminishes. To develop an insatiable hunger for Scripture we must feast on it regularly. At first, this may mean more discipline than desire. But don't give up. If you faithfully pursue a daily time in God's Word, the Holy Spirit will bless your obedience with a passion for Scripture. Soon your discipline will give way to desire. Donald S. Whitney offers this advice in his book, *Ten Questions to Diagnose Your Spiritual Health.* "One of the best ways for acquiring a taste for God's food and cultivating this Spirit-given appetite is simply to discipline yourself to feast on it. Nothing can make us hungry for Scripture more than Scripture itself."[8] If you are already in God's Word regularly, but your reading feels flat and routine, don't despair. A few changes to the way you approach the Bible can fire up your time in God's Word.

Begin the Feast

Maybe you have a sparse diet of God's Word — your time spent in the Bible is sporadic. Or perhaps you read Scripture consistently, almost daily, but you rarely sense God's presence. You lack passion for the Bible and its impact on your life is limited. You do not have to settle for weak, bland spiritual food. While only the Holy Spirit has the power to fire up your flat faith, you can take steps of obedience and position yourself to receive His blessings.

MAKE A COMMITMENT

If you want to fire up your flat faith, you must feast on God's Word. Remember our friend Ezra? His passion for God's Word satisfied his soul and filled his life with purpose. Ezra's devotion to Scripture was not halfhearted. He made an unwavering commitment to read and study it. He diligently pursued God through His revealed Word.

Today's society includes few examples of solid commitment. We change jobs, cities, and spouses as nonchalantly as we change clothes. Although commitment can be difficult to maintain, it produces benefits we cannot reap any other way. Recently, my parents celebrated their 50th wedding anniversary. There were certainly tears and struggles during those five decades, but as they cut the cake together at the big party, their love for each other was obvious.

Yes, sticking to a commitment to be in the Bible daily will be hard, especially at first. It requires discipline and sacrifice. You may have to adjust your schedule or give up something, but the benefits are eternally great. And as you practice the discipline of being in God's Word, your desire for it will grow. After a while, you will find that most days you sit down with the Bible because you *want* to, not because you *committed* to.

I experienced this myself. I made a commitment to obey God and seek Him in His Word. When I took that step of obedience, the Spirit began to create a longing in my heart. Although there are still days when I open the Bible out of obedience rather than desire, these are no longer the norm, but rather the exception. And God always blesses my obedience to be in His Word.

DEVELOP A PLAN

A haphazard approach to Bible intake will yield haphazard results. Time in the Bible must be planned and purposeful. Choose a reading plan that will be challenging but not overwhelming. If you don't already read your Bible several times a week, don't try to tackle the "Read the Whole Bible in a Year" plan. Evaluate where you are now and select a plan that is a step beyond that. Many plans schedule five days of reading a week, which gives you two days to "catch up." I occasionally have days when I let life take over and miss my time with God. You will too.

We also need a plan to *study* God's Word. This can be on our own, with a group, or both! Whatever your plan, be purposeful. Make a list of topics, Bible books, and characters that you want to know more about and then make a schedule to study them. Use study tools and dig deep. Too many Christians simply read God's Word and walk away with "what it means to me." But, what we *think* God's Word means is irrelevant. The only thing that matters is what *God* says it means. Simply reading God's Word is insufficient; we must study it too. Again, don't overwhelm yourself. Just take a step out from where you are now. There is a list of basic and very helpful study resources at the back of this book. We need to read seriously, in context, and applicationally. Start with one or two and add to your study library as you can! You can also access many great resources and tools online.

SAVOR AND SOAK

Earlier I told you I had been reading the Bible my entire life, but I had never absorbed it. Just as dry, cracked ground resists a fast, heavy deluge of water, God's Word simply ran off my parched soul. It was only when I began to savor, study, and contemplate Scripture that God's eternal truths began to soak into my heart.

We must slow down our intake of Scripture so its truths can penetrate the hard crust of our hearts. *Slow* does not mean "less frequently." Slow refers to our approach. Instead of continuing our often fast-paced, surface reading of God's Word, we must take the time to seriously contemplate what God is saying to us through His Word. Let's look at a few ways to do this.

Meditate on it:

The blessed man described in Psalm 1—the one who "delights in the Law of the LORD"—*meditates* on Scripture. There is a big difference between reading God's Word and meditating on it. Donald S. Whitney wrote about this distinction in *Ten Questions to Diagnose Your Spiritual Health*:

> Meditation (on God's Word) is the means of absorption. Spend 25 to 50 percent of your Bible intake time meditating on some verse, phrase, or word from your reading. Ask questions of it. Pray about it. Take your pen and scribble and doodle on a pad about it. Look for at least one way you could apply it. Linger over it. Soak your soul slowly in the water of the Word, and you'll find it not only refreshes you, but prompts a satisfying thirst for more.[9]

Meditation is not the emptying of your mind, but the filling of it with God's Word. Dwell on small nuggets of Scripture. Ask God to show you what it teaches about Him. Petition the Spirit to show you the eternal spiritual truths contained in it. Then determine how God wants you to act on it.

Pray it:

Scripture intake should always prompt prayer. As we read and meditate, we should continually respond to what God says to us. For instance, as we read Psalm 51:3—"For I know my transgressions"—the Holy Spirit may point out a specific sin we need to confess. Right then is the time for us to acknowledge our sin to God and repent.

Scripture can also *be* our prayer. No prayer is more eloquent or meaningful than God's own words. Start a list of passages you can use to pray in various life circumstances and for specific needs. For instance, I have a list of Scriptures about spiritual growth I use to pray for myself and others. Numerous resources are also available online and in Christian bookstores that will guide you in praying Scripture.

Memorize it:
I admit it. I struggle to memorize Scripture. Although I'm aware of the great benefits, I still balk at the discipline and hard work. A few years ago, God strongly convicted me about hiding His Word in my heart. I made a fresh commitment, developed a plan, and am making progress.

You may wonder why we need to memorize Scripture when we have such easy access to it. Memorizing God's Word solidly entrenches His truth in our hearts and minds. God then uses it to minister to us in powerful and very personal ways. If you have never memorized Scripture before, I suggest you begin with verses about God's great salvation. They will be a continual reminder of God's incredible grace. There are many solid resources on spiritual disciplines that can help you develop these areas. Check out the "Suggested Reading" list at the end of this book.

The Bible is God's primary catalyst for spiritual growth and deep soul satisfaction. If your faith is flat, if it is dry and brittle for lack of spiritual sustenance, then let God nourish your soul with the water of His Word. Sense His presence as you soak in Scripture. Spending time in God's Word is spending time with God Himself. I can't think of a better way to fire up flat, dry faith.

Chapter 9

GIVING GOD HIS DUE

Action #2: Connect with God in Worship

In order to join the Facebook group called the Anointed Michael Followers, you have to agree to this statement: "Michael Jackson is the Messiah." More than 500 people belong to this group and interact on the Facebook page. Although this is an extreme example, it's symptomatic of a widespread problem.

God wired us to worship Him. He formed us for His glory. He designed us to give Him honor and praise (Isaiah 43:7). We humans *will* worship. Unfortunately, in our fallen, sinful state we often withhold our worship from the only One who deserves it and give it away to something or someone that does not. Some cultures worship actual idols made of wood, stone, or metal. Other more "sophisticated" cultures like ours tend to worship money, success, relationships, or even other people. But when we worship the "created," we miss out on the sweet, intimate fellowship we can experience when we worship the Creator.

Wired to Worship

In chapter 6 we learned that we glorify or worship God with our lives as we obediently live for His purposes. The Apostle Paul writes about this *lifestyle* of worship in his letter to the Romans. "Therefore, I urge you, brothers, in view of God's mercy, to offer your bodies as living sacrifices, holy and pleasing to God—this is your spiritual act of worship" (Romans 12:1).

We also glorify God when we properly respond to Him with the *act* of worship. God created us with the ability to praise, honor, and adore Him for who He is. How often do you find yourself before God lost in worship? How often do you linger in His presence, simply enjoying the intimacy? My answer to both of those questions: "Not as much as I'd like." However, I do have those intimate moments—times when I wish the world would stop so I can remain in God's presence. But they are never long enough. I always want more.

If your faith feels flat and dry, evaluate the quality of your worship. A Christian who regularly brings the sacrifice of praise into God's presence will overflow with passion for her Creator. Here are a few questions to consider:

- Do you regularly sense your soul respond to the presence of God in your church's worship service?
- Does the worship of those around you in the service help ignite your worship?
- Do you purposefully praise God during your personal time with Him?
- Do you ever find yourself spontaneously responding to God in worship during the normal activities of the day?

Don't be discouraged if the questions above don't describe you. The goal of this chapter is to help us all worship God more often and more fully than we do now so we can enter His throne room and enjoy the sweet intimacy of His presence.

I know what's happening in heaven's throne room right now. Every creature is worshipping the Creator. The four living creatures covered with eyes and the 24 elders dressed in white are leading all of heaven's citizens in grand and glorious worship of the One who sits on the throne. They all fall down before Him and the elders lay their crowns before the throne. Constantly they praise Him:

> *Holy, holy, holy is the Lord God Almighty, who was, and is, and is to come. You are worthy, our Lord and God, to receive glory and honor and power, for you created all things, and by your will they were created and have their being* (Revelation 4:8, 11).

When God granted the Apostle John a glimpse into heaven, he discovered that the worship there never ceases, it continues "day and night" (Revelation 4:8). If you are a believer, worship is your eternal destiny. We were made to glorify—or worship—God (Isaiah 43:7). Worship is our earthly purpose—and our heavenly purpose.

Worthy of Worship

Since we will be worshipping God for all eternity, let's explore what "worship" means. In general, "worship" is a physical or outward expression of an inward attitude. It describes the homage paid by an inferior being to a superior being. With humility and reverence, a worshipper recognizes the worth of the object of worship. Worshippers often express their worship in physical ways such as kneeling or lying prostrate. These outward actions by themselves are not true worship, but they can reflect the inward attitudes of submission, reverence, and humility.

Specifically, Christian "worship" is recognizing and responding to the greatness and majesty of the one true God through His Son, Jesus. Christian worship acknowledges God's holy nature and reacts with profound awe. The skilled psalmist David beautifully described the foundation of worship in Psalm 29.

> *Ascribe to the LORD, O heavenly beings, ascribe to*
> *the LORD glory and strength.*
>   *Ascribe to the LORD the glory due his name;*
> *worship the LORD in the splendor of holiness.*
> (Psalm 29:1–2 ESV).

For 3,000 years David's psalm has been reminding God's people to give God His due. God deserves our worship because He is glorious and strong. God deserves our worship because His name is above all other names. God deserves our worship because He is splendid in His holiness.

True worship will always be expressed from inner attitudes such as humility, reverence, and submission. But it can also be demonstrated physically. When John saw the glorified Jesus, he "fell at his feet as though dead" (Revelation 1:17) and in the heavenly scene John described, the elders fell down before God and laid their crowns at His feet (Revelation 4:11).

Several different words have been translated as "worship" in the Bible. Interestingly, the original languages reveal a very close connection between "worship" and service and obedience. When Christians recognize the superior position and worth of God, our worship will go beyond attitudes. Our humble submission to God will produce obedience and service to Him and others.

Our obedience and service is the end result or outward fruit of worship. But God actually initiates worship. In John chapter 4, Jesus told the woman at the well that God seeks those who will worship Him in spirit and truth (John 4:23–24). God seeks us out and draws us to commune with Him in worship. Worship does not require a specific location, and it is not tied to a specific activity. Worship happens when our humble spirit hears God's call to recognize His worth. Our souls rise in praise, and we rejoice in the God of our salvation. True worship is a time of intimacy and fellowship with the object of our worship.

In an exposition of John 4, Scottish preacher, pastor, and university professor, Arthur John Gossip (1873–1954), elaborates on God's role in worship:

> Even when we are apathetic and half-hearted . . . God, with huge liberality in his heart and vast gifts in his hands, is searching for those who will accept them. . . . The central fact in a time of worship is not that we are seeking God, but that he is seeking us. But when God's willingness to give is met with responsive and receptive hearts; when what the liturgical experts call the descending type of service in which God comes to our aid with all the grace that we can need, intermingles with the ascending type, in which man climbs and reaches out toward God in adoration and thanksgiving, in confession and intercession and petition, with eager hearts that long for him and watch for him — things happen.[1]

Fruit of Worship

God seeks us. He is the initiator and the giver. He reaches down to meet with us, but He also bids us reach to Him with expectant hearts. And it is there in the meeting that "things happen." God addresses some of our deepest needs in times of worship. As we draw near to His throne we find mercy and grace (Hebrews 4:16). He heals hurts, eases grief, and pours out His peace. As we worship in His presence He fills us with joy (Psalm 16:11). And when believers connect with God in worship, He fuels our faith and reignites our passion for Him.

I especially feel close to God when everyday moments turn into times of worship. For instance, family hikes or camping provide the perfect opportunity for the beauty of God's creation to turn my heart toward Him. A colorful sunset, the power of the ocean, or snowcapped mountain peaks cause my soul to lift in worship to the Creator. But the absolute sweetest times have been when God took me completely by surprise.

Several years ago, I set aside a day to paint our bedroom. After gathering my drop cloths, ladder, rolling pans, and brushes, I got to work. For company, I tuned the radio to the local Christian music station. A few hours into the job, Michael W. Smith's song "Healing Rain" began to pour from the radio speakers. As I sang along, God called my heart toward His. There I stood in the middle of the room, dressed in paint-splattered clothes, with hands lifted high and tears flowing. The thickness of His presence took my breath away.

I didn't want that meeting with God to end. I would have remained until the paint dried. I did not manufacture that time, but I had practiced purposeful worship enough to recognize God's call to enjoy a priceless moment in His presence. I sang. I prayed. I lifted my hands and I bowed my knees. It was a sweet, precious time. And I would love to experience it more frequently.

Even though God initiates worship, we can make ourselves more open to His invitation. First, we can attune our ears to be more sensitive to His call. Reflect on previous times of worship. How did you sense God's presence? What where the circumstances that drew your attention to God? If you often sense God's presence when you read your Bible, then begin to practice purposeful praise during those times. If you are more sensitive to His presence during times of corporate worship, then work to limit anything that would distract during the service.

There may be times when you don't "feel" like worshipping. I've been there. But my obedience does not have to depend on my emotions. God calls me to worship and praise Him so I choose to obey. Often when I have stepped out in obedience and voiced praise to God, He met with me in that praise. He filled the moment with a sense of His presence. We don't have to wait on feelings to move toward worship.

The best way to cultivate feelings of worship is to increase our knowledge of God. Since worship is recognizing and responding to who God is, we can foster worship by knowing Him better. Theologian Wayne Grudem connects our knowledge of God with worship. "An attitude of worship comes upon us when we begin to see God as he is and then respond to his presence . . . genuine worship is not something that is self-generated or that can be worked up within ourselves. It must rather be the outpouring of our hearts *in response* to a realization of who God is."[2] Christians can expand our hearts for worship by expanding our knowledge of God. The more we know about God, the more we will respond to His holy nature in worship.

To Know the Unknowable

I made a new friend yesterday. I met Stephanie during the Bible study hour at church. Both our husbands were gone for the weekend so we sat next to each other during the service. Our afterchurch conversation turned into a decision to go to lunch. Soon, Stephanie and I were sharing our life stories over chips and salsa. We discovered that we both have daughters named Kelley and they are both expecting our first grandbabies.

Getting to know someone takes time. Even though Stephanie and I learned quite a bit about each other in a few hours, it will take a lot longer to know her well. Wayne and I have been married 28 years this month and know each other really well. Not long ago he was with me when I went to pick out a new case for my cell phone. I knew what his opinion would be about each one even before I showed it to him. The look on his face simply confirmed it. When I made my choice I handed it to the clerk and said, "My husband thinks it's gaudy." The clerk smiled uncomfortably and Wayne grinned and nodded.

When two people spend almost three decades together they tend to know each other backward and forward. They know how the other will react in a given situation and what they think about almost everything. I can truthfully say I know my husband. (I do admit that on the very rare occasion he surprises me.) Human beings have the capability of knowing and understanding each other. We are made of the same stuff.

However, humans are incapable of *completely* knowing God. We are limited, finite creatures. God is infinite and inscrutable. Even if God fully explained Himself to us, our minds could not comprehend it. The more I study and think about who God is, the more I realize I cannot deeply grasp Him. Yet, acknowledging that truth presses my heart even closer to worship. For if I could fully understand Him, then He would not be worthy of worship.

We cannot find out about God on our own. He is incomprehensible to the human mind. But we can know what the Spirit of God chooses to make known to us (1 Corinthians 2:10–16). In his book *The Knowledge of the Holy*, A. W. Tozer elaborates:

> "What is God like? If by that question we mean
> "What is God like in Himself?" there is no answer.

If we mean "What has God disclosed about Himself that the reverent reason can comprehend?" there is, I believe, an answer both full and satisfying. For while the name of God is secret and His essential nature incomprehensible, He in condescending love has by revelation declared certain things to be true of Himself.[3]

Getting to Know Him

Although we are incapable of fully knowing and understanding God, we can know what He has chosen to reveal about Himself. God has disclosed Himself to us in several ways. First, He has revealed His existence and power in a general way through creation.

> For the wrath of God is revealed from heaven against all ungodliness and unrighteousness of men, who by their unrighteousness suppress the truth. For what can be known about God is plain to them, because God has shown it to them. For his invisible attributes, namely, his eternal power and divine nature, have been clearly perceived, ever since the creation of the world, in the things that have been made. So they are without excuse (Romans 1:18–20 ESV).

God has clearly made His existence known through the created world. Mankind has no excuse for ignoring the truth of God's existence because the very existence of the world proves that He is. The created order also testifies to God's divine attributes like His power and authority. We can learn a lot about the nature of God by considering what He has made. For instance, think about the vast array of plant and animal life. Everything from the giraffe and platypus to the Venus flytrap and California redwood demonstrate God's creativity. The seed within the apple and the perfect distance of the earth from the sun point to God's care and provision.

Begin to look at the world with new eyes. Become an observer with the goal of learning more about the Creator. Take note of the order and detail. Each bird in flight and every rainbow on the horizon declares the glory of God. Pay attention to God's creation. The next time something amazing catches your eye, remember the One who made it. When you reflect on the beauty around you, accept the Creator's invitation to worship. Praise Him for His power and creativity. Thank Him for His provision. Give the Creator His due.

God has also chosen to make Himself known to us through His written Word. The Bible is so deep and rich, we can spend our lives reading and studying it and still not grasp everything it reveals to us about God. Scripture displays God's holy nature and describes it with attributes we will recognize. We learn that God is loving, merciful, just, gracious, kind, patient, forgiving, jealous, and much more. The Bible also depicts God's ways and presents His will. A student of the Bible can gain knowledge of the way God works in this world and in the lives of His people. For instance, we learn to rest in the truth that absolutely nothing happens in our lives without God's knowledge and permission. And we also discover our need for a Savior and comprehend God's great provision through Christ.

A thorough knowledge of the God of Scripture requires more than simply showing up on Sunday morning and hearing what someone else has learned. While biblical preaching and teaching is vital for the building up of the body, it is not enough. Every Christian must be purposeful in our approach to Scripture. In the last chapter we discussed in length the great spiritual benefits of reading and studying God's Word. If you missed that chapter, or it's been a while since you read it, take a few minutes to review it. It includes encouragement and helpful direction for reading and studying the Bible. Learning about the God of the Bible is a life-long journey, so there's no time to waste.

The most exciting way God has revealed Himself to us is through His Son. The author of Hebrews said that the Son is "the radiance of the glory of God and the exact imprint of his nature" (Hebrews 1:3 ESV). Jesus told His disciples that "whoever has seen me has seen the Father" (John 14:9 ESV). We can learn *about* the Father by studying the character and ways of the Son, but we can also personally *know* God through a believing relationship with Jesus.

Jesus defines eternal life as knowing Him and His Father. "Now this is eternal life; that they may know you, the only true God, and Jesus Christ, who you have sent" (John 17:3). If you are a believer in Jesus, you have a personal relationship with the Creator of the universe. You can know *about* Him and you can *know* Him.

My husband, Wayne, admires the well-known actor John Wayne. He half-jokingly suggested we name our son John Wayne and call him Duke for short. Wayne has read about his life and has seen all his movies. But the story he tells with excitement is about the time he *almost* shook the Duke's hand at a football game. About to pass each other in the stadium, Mr. Wayne's eyes connected with my Wayne's. The Duke extended his hand, but before they reached each other an assistant called him away. Mr. Wayne tipped his hat to my future husband and turned on the heel of his boot. Almost. Anybody can know *about* someone important, but *personal knowledge* requires relationship.

We don't have to settle for knowing *about* God. We don't have to be satisfied with a distant, impersonal knowledge of Him. We can know Him personally, even intimately. Those who have never repented of their sins and put their trust in Jesus as their Savior can only know *about* God. No matter how much they study the Bible, they cannot know God personally. But those of us who have entered into a saving relationship with Jesus can follow Him into the very throne room of God. Jesus, our High Priest, has provided access to the Father through His own body (Hebrews 10:19–22). We can enter God's presence and draw near to Him in worship.

Does that amazing truth overwhelm you? It should. In fact, it should knock us to our knees in humility. We do not deserve the incredible privilege of worshipping in God's presence. Yet, the blood of Christ makes this possible. The ability to worship in God's presence is a glorious privilege earned for us by Jesus. Simply thinking about the access we have to God through Christ should turn our hearts to worship.

Do you take the privilege of worship for granted? I know there have been times in my life when I did. It's no coincidence that those were times when my faith was a bit on the flat side. But flat faith can be fired up by regularly entering God's presence in worship. In those precious times we experience intimate fellowship with God. Through that fellowship He meets our deepest needs and fills us with His joy.

In this chapter, we've explored several ways to foster worship in our lives. First, be sensitive to God's invitation to worship. Second, become an observer of the Creator by observing His creation. Third, commit to learning more about our worthy God through His Word. Fourth, reflect on the amazing privilege of personally knowing God through Jesus. Finally, enter into His presence with humble submission ready to receive everything He has to offer.

Chapter 10

SPARKS OF OBEDIENCE

Action #3: Obey God to Experience His Blessings

A couple of years ago, our teenage son, Mark, adopted an abandoned puppy. It was an unplanned adoption. The Saturday in October that we stopped at the pet store for dog food just happened to be "adopt a pet" day. The rescue society had pens all over the store full of furry-faced, big-eyed mutts, each one begging to be taken home. Mark, who quickly fell for an energetic terrier mix, soon began doing some begging of his own.

I had no intention of letting Mark have that dog. Training a new puppy requires a lot of work and persistence. And of course I suspected who would be cleaning up the majority of the potty mistakes. But Mark made all kinds of big promises about how diligent he would be. And he successfully made me feel guilty about the fact that his two sisters each had dogs of their own. So I agreed to ask a few questions.

We learned as much as we could about the puppy from the society volunteer. He had been discovered in the fenced back yard of the city pound early one morning. His broken leg led them to believe he had just been dropped over the tall fence. In addition to his injury, he had worms and kennel cough. They had treated everything and he was ready to be adopted. After a quick phone call to my husband, Mark announced, "Dad didn't say no!" At that point what else could I do?

We took the dog home and Mark named him Remi. If you've ever had a puppy, you know what came next — all-night whining, endless toilet accidents, shoe chewing, and finger-nipping. Mark was determined to work with Remi until he was an obedient, well-trained pet. We took the usual precautions to protect the house and other property from puppy pee and sharp, little teeth. Remi stayed in his kennel unless a family member was actively watching him. We took him outside at regular intervals, encouraging him with "Remi, potty!" and "Good boy!" Then, little by little, as Remi's behavior improved he earned more and more freedom.

The discipline Remi had the most trouble with was coming when called. If we were inside, he did pretty well. But if he got the chance to escape through the front door or out the back gate, we had to chase him down. One cool night the little mutt dashed out the front door when my father-in-law opened it to leave. I called for Mark who ran out of his room wearing nothing but gym shorts. Mark shot out the front door hollering, "Remi, come!"

From my relaxed position in the recliner in the living room I could see a small rectangle of the front yard through the open door. First the mutt flashed past. Then the bare-footed, shirtless boy flashed past. "Remi, come!" Then the mutt sped by going the opposite direction. Then the boy sped by. "Remi, come!" This continued for several minutes until Mark finally managed to tackle the mutt in the grass.

Now, Remi is thoroughly house-broken. He does not chew shoes or furniture. He obediently responds to "sit," "stay," and "play dead." He is sweet and loving. He no longer has to sleep in his kennel. We can leave him in the house unsupervised. But after two years we still cannot take him into the front yard unless he is on a leash. It's a big, wide world out there and he will make a run for it.

Remi's obedience has resulted in blessings. He sleeps on Mark's bed. He gets to wander the house as he pleases. He hangs out with the family. He has his own blanket and chew toys and more treats than he needs. But his area of disobedience keeps him from enjoying certain privileges. He has to stay in the house if we step out front. If the backyard gates need to be opened, Remi has to be held or put in his kennel. Obedience brings blessings. Disobedience not only brings discipline, but it also restricts blessings.

If you are struggling with flat faith, if you feel you are missing out on some of the blessings of a relationship with Christ, then perhaps it's time to check your level of obedience to God. As we discussed in chapter 3, we are not saved *by* good works, but God does save us *for* good works. He expects us to obey His commands and live holy lives. Scripture teaches that God disciplines His children's disobedience and blesses our obedience. Evangelical Christians often hesitate to stress God's blessings for obedience. We do not want to risk clouding the glorious truth that we are saved solely by God's mercy and grace and not by anything we do. Unfortunately, because we are often overly cautious, we fail to stress God's call to obedience, and in the process, neglect the exciting news that we will experience God's activity and blessing when we obey. In this chapter, we will highlight some of God's conditional promises and see how obedience can send sparks to our dry faith.

A Mountain of Blessings

The covenant renewal ceremony between God and the nation of Israel in Joshua 8 is an unusual scene that demonstrates the spiritual truth that God blesses obedience. After 40 years of wandering in the wilderness, the Israelites finally entered the Promised Land. Now they stood in the valley between Mount Gerizim and Mount Ebal to fulfill the instructions Moses gave them before he died (Deuteronomy 27:1 to 28:68). First, Joshua built an altar of uncut stones and they offered sacrifices to God. Next, Joshua wrote all God's laws on large stones and set them up on Mount Ebal. Then the people divided themselves. Half the tribes stood on Mount Ebal and the other half on Mount Gerizim.

Joshua read all the blessings for obedience and curses for disobedience as prescribed in the law. Those who stood on Mount Ebal represented the curses. Each time Joshua pronounced a curse for disobedience those standing on Mount Ebal said "Amen!" "'Cursed be anyone who misleads a blind man on the road.' And all the people shall say, 'Amen'" (Deuteronomy 27:18 ESV). Curse after curse was read.

In contrast, those who stood on Mount Gerizim represented the blessings.

> *"And if you faithfully obey the voice of the* LORD *your God, being careful to do all his commandments that I command you today, the* LORD *your God will set you high above all the nations of the earth. And all these blessings shall come upon you and overtake you, if you obey the voice of the* LORD *your God"* (Deuteronomy 28:1–2 ESV).

God's promises for blessings included victory in battle, plentiful crops, and a unique relationship with Him. If they obeyed. If they didn't obey, they would experience His discipline.

Can you picture this amazing scene? Two mountains. A sea of people. A solemn ceremony. The reading of a long list of blessings and curses—all dependent on the people's level of obedience. God was serious about Israel obeying His commands. Obedience brings blessings, and He wanted His people to thrive in their new home.

Many of God's promised blessings in Scripture were conditional on the obedience of His people. For instance, in Exodus 19, when God revealed Himself to the nation of Israel on Mount Sinai, He made this conditional promise:

> *Then Moses climbed the mountain to appear before God. The LORD called to him from the mountain and said, "Give these instructions to the family of Jacob; announce it to the descendants of Israel: 'You have seen what I did to the Egyptians. You know how I carried you on eagles' wings and brought you to myself. Now if you will obey me and keep my covenant, you will be my own special treasure from among all the peoples on earth; for all the earth belongs to me. And you will be my kingdom of priests, my holy nation.' This is the message you must give to the people of Israel"* (Exodus 19:3–6 NLT).

The covenant of relationship God first established with Abraham and the patriarchs was *unconditional*. God would indeed give the Promised Land to Abraham's descendants and bless the entire earth through his seed. On Mount Sinai, God reiterated and expanded this unconditional covenant with the nation of Israel. But certain aspects of the relationship heavily depended on their obedience.

God promised the Israelites they would be His special treasure, a nation of priests, and a holy nation—*if*. If they obeyed Him. If they kept His covenant. These conditional blessings concerned the level of intimacy they would experience with God and their usefulness for His purposes. If they obeyed, they would enjoy a deep and fulfilling relationship with God. If they obeyed, they would be the kind of people God could use to reach the world. If they obeyed.

Count Your Blessings

The Bible contains many glorious, *unconditional* promises of God. But scores of wonderful, *conditional* promises also fill God's Word. I don't want to miss out on anything God wants to give me because of my failure to obey. What about you?

Before we look at what the Bible says about God's blessings for obedience, I want to highlight what it does *not* say. The Bible does not teach that obedient Christians will never have problems. Scripture does not say that God will always fill the lives of faithful believers with health, wealth, and material prosperity. In fact, the Bible clearly teaches that believers will most certainly face difficult times and endure all kinds of trials. Paul wrote to Timothy that believers who live a godly life will be persecuted (2 Timothy 3:12). Peter, James, and Paul all taught that God allows trials into the lives of Christians to strengthen and refine our faith (1 Peter 1:6–7; James 1:2-4; Romans 5:3–5).

God may choose to bless you with health and wealth to be used for His purposes. However, God also allows illness, trials, and financial difficulties into the lives of many faithful Christians. Let's take a look at a few promised blessings for obedience God does make in His Word.

- Those who trust in the Lord will not have to worry when hard times come (Jeremiah 17:7–8).
- Those who live holy lives will enjoy a deeper intimacy with God (Matthew 5:8; John 15:9–10; Isaiah 59:2).

- God will reveal Himself to those who obey His commands (John 14:21).
- Those who obediently live by the Spirit will produce the fruit of the Spirit (Galatians 5:16–26).
- The obedient will enjoy a clear conscience before God (Romans 13:5; 1 Timothy 1:18–19).
- Those who live holy lives are more productive and effective in God's work. (2 Timothy 2:20–21).
- God will be attentive to the prayers of the obedient (Psalm 66:18; 1 Peter 3:12; 1 John 3:22).

Did you notice the spiritual nature of these promises? This list was just a sampling of the blessings God promises to those of His children who respond to Him with obedience. When I began searching the Bible, I was a little shocked at the number and scope of God's *conditional* blessings. Our salvation does not depend on adhering to God's commands, but the quality of our relationship with Him certainly does. If you feel disconnected from God, if your faith feels weak, flat and dry, part of the solution is to evaluate your obedience.

How would you rate your obedience? Perhaps you say yes to the big things but tend to overlook the small, seemingly insignificant things. Or maybe you follow God faithfully in matters that require little risk and hold back on the big stuff. Obedience in every area of life, big and small — whether we understand or don't understand God's purpose behind the command — will build our faith.

In his challenging classic *The Cost of Discipleship*, German pastor Dietrich Bonhoeffer wrote about the connection between obedience and faith.

> No one should be surprised at the difficulty of faith,
> if there is some part of his life where he is consciously
> resisting or disobeying the commandment of Jesus.
> Is there some part of your life which you are refusing
> to surrender at his behest, some sinful passion,
> maybe, or some animosity, some hope, perhaps
> your ambition or reason? If so, you must not be
> surprised that you have not received the Holy Spirit,
> that prayer is difficult, or that your request for faith
> remains unanswered. Go rather and be reconciled
> with your brother, renounce the sin which holds you
> fast—and then you will recover your faith! If you
> dismiss the word of God's command, you will not
> receive his word of grace. How can you hope to enter
> into communion with him when at some point in
> your life you are running away from him?[1]

Is there some area of your life in which you have been less than
fully obedient to God? Perhaps God has been whispering to you
to obey Him for a long time. It may be a stronghold of sin that
directly contradicts God's Word. Perhaps He has asked you to serve
in some area, but you have held back in favor of other priorities.
Maybe it's a relationship that needs mending or an addiction that
needs breaking or an attitude that needs changing. Will you choose
obedience today? Obey and embrace God's conditional blessings.

From Dry to Flaming in One Step

Not everyone's flat faith is a result of continued disobedience.
However, purposeful, active obedience can ignite new passion for
Christ. Each act of obedience is a spark that can set dry faith on fire.

In chapter 1, I told you about my friend Connie Cavanaugh, who spent ten years kicking up sand in a spiritual wilderness. This pastor's wife—once on fire for Christ—pretended everything was fine while in reality her faith felt dry and dead. Finally, in desperation, she threw down a gauntlet before God. In the first real prayer she'd prayed in a long time she told God she would follow Him, but He would have to come after her first because she didn't know where to find Him. What Connie didn't realize is that God had been waiting for her willingness to obey.

Connie's opportunity for obedience came not long after with an invitation to speak at a women's retreat across the county. Immediately she remembered her desperate prayer and realized this could be her first step of obedience out of her spiritual drought. This yes was just the beginning of a whole series of yeses that set her on a course of following God out of the wilderness and into a place of spiritual bounty. In her second book, *Following God One Yes at a Time,* Connie writes about the importance of obedience.

> There is an important element I learned the hard way, and I don't want you to miss it. It's difficult to hear from God if you're not following Him. It's so easy to get caught up in the world and what's happening that you simply miss God's voice . . . or misunderstand Him. . . . When God points you in a certain direction, say yes with your feet. One simple, immediate, possible yes leads to another, and another, as you obey His directives. . . . When you move, you'll begin to hear Him more clearly. Why? One simple reason: You have put yourself in a place where you can't make it without Him. . . . The absolutely best place to hear from God is while you're

moving forward to achieve the dream because you
are in the center of His will.[2]

One step of obedience can start your relationship with Jesus on
a whole new trajectory. Luke chapter 5 records an encounter
between Jesus and Peter that illustrates this truth. One morning
as Jesus taught on the shore of the Sea of Galilee, the growing
crowd pressed against Him. Nearby, fishermen who had just
returned from their night of fishing were washing their nets at the
water's edge. Jesus climbed into one of the boats, which belonged
to Simon Peter, and asked him to push out a little from the shore
so he could teach from a better vantage point.

When Jesus finished teaching, He gave Peter some unusual
instructions. "Now go out where it is deeper and let down your
nets, and you will catch many fish" (Luke 5:4 NLT). I can just
imagine what Peter and the other fishermen were thinking. They
had been fishing all night without catching a single fish. They
were the skilled fishermen. This was their trade. If the fish were
biting, then they would have caught them. But that's not how
Peter responded to Jesus. "Master," Simon replied, "we worked
hard all last night and didn't catch a thing. But if you say so, we'll
try again" (Luke 5:5 NLT).

So Peter and his partners put out to deep water. The catch was
so large their freshly cleaned nets began to tear and the boat was
in danger of sinking. They even had to call for another boat to
come help bring in the fish. Peter, overwhelmed with the power
of Christ, fell to his knees in repentance and worship. When they
returned to shore, Peter left his nets, his boat, and the fish to
follow Jesus.

One step of obedience completely turned Peter's life around.
Why? Through that one act of obedience, God revealed Himself to

Peter in a fresh, awe-inspiring way. Peter could have told Jesus that he was just too tired to let the nets down again. After all, it didn't make any sense. Peter could have asked Jesus to come back later that evening. That was the appropriate time for fishing anyway. Peter could have politely told Jesus that He really didn't know best. Peter was the fisherman.

But Peter obeyed. Even though he was tired, Peter obeyed. Even though it made no sense, Peter obeyed. Even though he was the fisherman, Peter obeyed. Even though the timing seemed off, Peter obeyed. And because he obeyed, Peter witnessed the power of God. That one step of obedience changed his life forever.

Blessings for Obedience

What experiences with God have you missed because you failed to take one step of obedience? I don't mean to imply that one single step of obedience will always radically change your life like that one act changed Peter's, but it can. However, obedience does deepen our relationship with God and puts us in a position to experience His activity and power. And disobedience separates us from many of God's blessings.

In chapter 6, I told you how God equipped me and involved me in teaching the Bible to spiritual seekers. One particularly exciting thing happened during that very first study that required me to take an unusual step of obedience. Sandy was one of the four women in that first group. Late one afternoon the thought popped into my head to call Sandy. It was not the most convenient time for me. My parents were visiting from out-of-town and I was cooking dinner for the family. But the thought persisted and I soon determined it must be from God. I also got the impression this would be no normal, casual phone call. God wanted me to give Sandy the opportunity to accept Christ as her Savior.

At first I balked. "What? Share the gospel and ask for a response over the phone? Isn't that a bit impersonal?" But God persisted and I picked up the phone. Sandy was at home and answered quickly. She was glad I called. In fact, her toddler was down for a nap and it was the "perfect time." We chatted for a few minutes, and then I asked her how she liked the Bible study. We talked about what we had been studying and God brought our conversation around to salvation. I jumped in. "Sandy, would you like to give your life to Jesus?" Her response: "Yes, can I do it right now?!"

God knew exactly what He was doing. He didn't need me to carry out His plan to save Sandy, but I was so blessed to be a witness to His awesome activity. If I had not obeyed His strange prompting that afternoon, I would have missed it. I admit I don't always obey Him in cases like that. But when I do He always blesses me.

Is God prompting you to take a step of obedience? It might seem insignificant or impossible. Maybe it's something small you've been putting off until a "convenient" time. As we've seen in this chapter, God blesses obedience. When we don't obey, we separate ourselves from so many of His promises. If you want to fire up your flat faith, then take a step of obedience. Join God in His plans. Put yourself out there. Then stand back and watch the sparks fly.

Chapter 11

FAMILY TIES

Action #4: Stay Vitally Connected to a Local Church

The call came from my father-in-law right after dinner. He and Wayne's mom had been in a car accident. He had suffered some cuts and bruises. She was with Jesus.

We had seen them two weeks earlier for Christmas when we made the 2,000-mile trek from where we lived in Alberta, Canada, to their home in Louisiana. Now the distance seemed insurmountable. We would leave as quickly as possible but so many things had to be done. The first thing I did was call my friend Susan. Twenty minutes later the house began to fill up with loving members of our church family.

Immediately they began to take care of us. Connie spent two hours on the phone with the airline making reservations and securing the compassion fare. Steve gathered the Sunday School material so he could teach Wayne's class. Susan got needed dress clothes for our son, Mark. Jimmy arranged to take us to the airport. Others handled the dog, the house, and countless responsibilities we simply could not walk away from. And in the midst of all the activity there were prayers, hugs, and tears. Within hours we were ready to travel.

In Louisiana, my father-in-law encountered the same love and care from his church family. Friends went to the hospital to bring him home. Two men stayed with him throughout that first night after the accident. Some of the women made sure the beds were ready for us. By the time we arrived the kitchen and refrigerator were filled with food. No need went unmet.

Have you ever had a similar experience with your church family? Not everyone has. Many Christians have been hurt by people in the church. I've been hurt more than once, and I know how hard it can be to move past that hurt. But more importantly, I've been overwhelmed with love from the church. As we will see in this chapter, learning to give and receive the love of Christ in the context of His church is a vital component of fueling and sustaining our faith.

What's the Big Deal?

Ironically, as I write this, I am "churchless." Recently we moved clear across the state of Texas for my husband's job. When we left the desert of west Texas for Houston, we also left our church family. I've been in this situation before and I really, really don't like it. We've moved seven times in 28 years of marriage. Each time we left a city we also had to leave our spiritual family. Over the years, each network of Christian friends cared for us, loved us, encouraged us, and challenged us. (Did I mention that I really, really don't like leaving that family behind?)

However, we won't be churchless for long. Even before all the boxes were unpacked, we began visiting churches in the area. We never feel fully settled into a new home until we are settled into a local church family. As soon as God confirms where He wants us, we will join and begin to serve. A vital connection to a local church is not optional for us for two reasons. The first reason is purely selfish. We need the church for our own happiness and spiritual well-being. The second reason is because we want to obey God and serve His people.

Why is a local church so important? Faith in Christ is intrinsically communal. God designed our life of discipleship to be one of interdependence. Each believer is dependent on the larger group of believers to receive much of what God desires to give us and do in us. Over and over in the New Testament we see the phrase "one another" to refer to the nature of the relationship between believers. On the night Jesus was arrested, one of the last things He told the disciples was to love each other as He loved them. "A new commandment I give to you, that you love one another: just as I have loved you, you also are to love one another" (John 13:34 ESV). Jesus' command reveals His plan to show love to the individual believer through the community of believers.

The Greek verb translated as "love" in John 13:34 corresponds to the Greek noun *agape*. It's the same kind of love God showed for the world when He sent Jesus to die for our sins (John 3:16). Agape love always expresses itself in action. "But God shows his love for us in that while we were still sinners, Christ died for us" (Romans 5:8 ESV). This is the kind of love God commands us to have for each other—unselfish, sacrificial love in action. Agape love involves much more than our emotions. It is a product of our mind and will. Therefore, we can choose to love others like God loves us. We don't have to wait on feelings, we can purposefully move forward and show our love through actions.

Because of God's love for us, we should also love our fellow Christians.

> "Dear friends, since God loved us that much, we surely ought to love each other. No one has ever seen God. But if we love each other, God lives in us, and his

love has been brought to full expression through us"
(1 John 4:11-12 NLT).

The way we show our gratitude and love for God is by loving His children. When we obey His command to love our fellow Christians, we in turn are blessed with God's love. God loves us through "one another." And this love is to be expressed in the context of the church.

Believers express their love to one another in various ways. If you were to do a quick search of the expression "one another" in the New Testament, you would discover a host of ways God commands us to show our love to each other in the church. Here's a sampling:

- Honor one another (Romans 12:10).
- Teach God's Word to one another (Romans 15:14).
- Comfort one another (2 Corinthians 13:11).
- Serve one another (Galatians 5:13; 1 Peter 4:10).
- Restore one another (Galatians 6:1).
- Bear one another's burdens (Galatians 6:2).
- Forgive one another (Ephesians 4:32).
- Build up one another (1 Thessalonians 5:11).
- Do good to one another (1 Thessalonians 5:15).
- Exhort one another (Hebrews 3:13).
- Encourage one another to do good deeds (1 Thessalonians 4:18; Hebrews 10:24).
- Meet one another's physical needs (James 2:15–17; 1 John 3:17).
- Pray for one another to be healed (James 5:16).
- Show hospitality to one another (1 Peter 4:9).

God uses local believers to encourage us, meet our needs, comfort us, teach us, and fellowship with us. God shows His love to us through believers in a local church. In their book *Experiencing God*

Together, Henry and Melvin Blackaby emphasize the corporate nature of our faith.

> Just as God designed for a baby to be born into a family to receive love and care, so He designed for those who are "born again" to enter a spiritual family that will love and care for them. There is a corporate dimension to the nature of God's great salvation that is at the heart of God's purpose for each individual Christian. Without a thorough understanding of our place in the family of God, we will experience a dysfunctional Christian life.[1]

God has chosen to work through the church to bless His children. If we are not connected in relationship with a body of believers, we will miss out on so much of what God wants to give us.

You Aren't Fine Without It

The Bible also teaches that we can never be all God saved us to be without being vitally connected to a local church. We can understand this better by taking a closer look at the nature of the church. Jesus is the founder and Head of the church. The Greek word translated as "church" in Matthew 16:18, records Jesus' words: "I will build my church." It is *ekklesia.* It refers to a congregation or assembly of individuals that have been "called out." So, by definition, "church" is people called out by God. Do you remember that old rhyme we used to do with hand motions? *Here's the church; here's the steeple; open the door, and here's all the people.* Cute and fun to do with our kids, but it's just plain wrong. That's not what the Bible teaches about the church. Church is not a building. It's not the activities we go to on Sunday morning. The church is the people of God.

The Bible uses numerous metaphors to help us understand God's purpose for the church. One of my favorites is the Church is God's household (1 Timothy 3:15). God is our Father, Jesus is our Brother, and believers are all brothers and sisters through our relationship with Jesus (Matthew 12:48–50; 2 Corinthians 6:18; 1 John 3:14–15; and 1 Timothy 5:1–2). This picture of family helps us grasp the relationship of love God intends for the church.

The metaphor that best demonstrates the interdependent nature of the church is found in the fourth chapter of Ephesians. The Apostle Paul wrote that the church is one "body," with one God and Father, and Jesus is the Head (Ephesians 4:4–6). God gifts and uses individual believers to benefit the body as a whole.

> *Now these are the gifts Christ gave to the church: the apostles, the prophets, the evangelists, and the pastors and teachers. Their responsibility is to equip God's people to do his work and build up the church, the body of Christ. This will continue until we all come to such unity in our faith and knowledge of God's Son that we will be mature in the Lord, measuring up to the full and complete standard of Christ. Then we will no longer be immature like children. We won't be tossed and blown about by every wind of new teaching. We will not be influenced when people try to trick us with lies so clever they sound like the truth. Instead, we will speak the truth in love, growing in every way more and more like Christ, who is the head of his body, the church. He makes the whole body fit together perfectly. As each part does its own special work, it helps the other parts grow, so that the whole body is healthy and growing and full of love.* (Ephesians 4:11–16 NLT).

God's goal is to grow and mature individual believers together as a whole. As each member uses her gift to fulfill the role in the body God gave her, all the members will become more and more like Christ, the Head. Your full and complete spiritual growth and maturity depends on the other members of the body obeying God. And their growth and maturity depends on yours. This passage from Ephesians also shows the spiritual protection we gain from being connected to a church. We are far less likely to be swayed by inaccuracies or led away from Christ by false teaching. We must embrace this symbiotic relationship with other believers to become all God wants us to become and to receive everything God wants to give us.

Even though the teaching of Scripture is clear, statistics reveal that many Christians fail to see the importance of the church to their faith. A 2007 study by the Barna Group estimates that 13 to 15 million Americans who say they have a personal, saving relationship with Christ, can be defined as "unchurched." Barna uses the term *unchurched* to describe people who have "not attended a religious service of any type during the past six months."[2] According to this study, millions of Americans who profess Christ as their Savior have no real relationship with a local church. They do not feel church is important to their faith. How do you feel about the church? Jesus loved her enough to die for her (Ephesians 5:25–27). Christ purchased the church with His own blood (Acts 20:28) so He could "rescue us from this evil age" (Galatians 1:4). If the church is that important to Jesus, then it should be important to us.

Wayne and I can't wait to find the local church body God has for us. One amazing thing about being Christians is that wherever we go, some of God's family is already there waiting for us. Each time we've moved we have had an instant connection to people because we have the same Father. We have the purposes of God in common. We share the love of Christ. Right now, as we work to find that new church home, God comforts me in the truth that He has a place picked out for us already. He knows what our role in that church family will be. He knows how He will use us in their lives and how He will use them in our lives.

Finding Your Place

Are you connected to a local church? Are you experiencing the kind of church relationship Paul wrote about in Ephesians chapter 4? Some Christians rarely, if ever, attend church. Other believers only attend church on Sunday morning and wonder why they aren't experiencing the symbiotic relationship God intends. Real connection requires more than mere attendance or having your name on a membership roll. Vital connection to a church body must include fellowship and service.

How do you get started? If you are not a member of a local church, the first step is to join one. Begin visiting churches near your home. God has placed you in your community and wants to use you there. Don't drive past dozens of churches strictly because another one miles away has a popular, dynamic personality in the pulpit. Make sure the church's preaching and teaching is accurate to God's Word. Check the church's Web site for a statement of beliefs. Ask questions about how the church is involved in the community and missions. Find out the church's needs. Be sensitive to God's prompting. He has a church for you. He has equipped you to serve in a local church. He will show you where He wants you to be.

If you are a member of a local church, have you found your place of service? Remember, God's design for the church includes a reciprocal relationship between its members. Every member receives from the body, but also gives to the body. Unfortunately, many local churches suffer from Christian "parasites." These believers take spiritual nourishment, encouragement, and support from the body but give nothing back. This kind of relationship not only harms the church body, it also harms that individual Christian. Unless every member uses the gifts God gave them to build up that body, the local church cannot be everything God wants it to be. Thus, the individual members will not receive everything God wants to give.

Find your place of service. Evaluate the gifts, talents, and life experiences God has given you. We discussed this in depth in chapter 6. Review that chapter if needed to get a good grasp on how God has equipped you to serve Him and His church. Talk to the pastor and other leaders about areas of need in the church. Where do they need help? Are there ministries they would like to begin, but they need the right person to lead out? Ask God to show you how His equipping matches the needs of your church. When He shows you, step in and get serving.

Sometimes the hardest way to connect to your church is in the area of fellowship. God wants the members of His church to walk through life together. Many of those "one anothers" we mentioned can only happen in the context of friendship. The New Testament believers not only met together for worship and the teaching of the Word, they also prayed together, ate together, hung out together, and met each other's needs (Acts 2:42–47). This doesn't happen during just two hours on Sunday morning.

How do we connect with other believers in our church in friendship? I wish I could tell you that if you simply show up and get involved others will always reach out to you. Sometimes it happens like that, but often it does not. We have experienced it both ways. When we moved to Casper, Wyoming, in 1988, we began to look for the church God had for us there. One Sunday night we visited one of the churches in town. Our oldest child was just 18 months old so we took her to the nursery for the service. When we picked her up afterwards, another young couple was picking up their son. They introduced themselves and we chatted for a few minutes. Before we left the church that night we had plans for Friday night. Lloyd and Becky became our first friends in Casper. They introduced us to other young couples in the church and we quickly found our place of fellowship and friendship.

I could tell you similar stories from other moves. But a few times we moved we had to be the ones to reach out and initiate friendship. Sometimes people have allowed themselves to become too busy and don't take the time for the more important things. Other times people—yes, even Christians—are too inwardly focused to notice that someone needs a friend. Don't be afraid to invite someone out for coffee or over for dinner. Wayne and I have often taken the initiative in a new church.

Often, the bigger the church, the harder it is to develop friendships. It's easy to get lost in the crowd. If you belong to a large church, make sure you are part of a small group too, such as a Sunday School class, home group, or ministry team. Find your place of service in the body of Christ, reach out to the members God has placed around you, and begin to experience the blessings of God's family.

Getting Past the Hurt

Maybe you're missing out on the blessings of God's church because you've been hurt in the past. I know what it's like to be hurt by those you love and trust. But if we allow the past to prevent us from being vitally connected to a church, we are merely continuing to hurt ourselves. I do not know your situation. I do not know the exact nature of those things that hurt you. But I do know that God does not want any betrayal, rejection, deception, violation, or injury—no matter how ugly or deep—to keep you from His church.

First, remember that God did not hurt you. People hurt you. They may have acted "in the name of God," but their sin was not ordained by Him. Every local church is comprised of redeemed but imperfect people. God knows it and He still chooses to work in the church and through the church to accomplish His purposes. Some local churches do exist that are far away from God in word or deed, but you can find one that loves God and desires to follow Him. Please don't miss out on experiencing God because of what another person did.

Once I was hurt when no one in our church responded to what I felt to be an urgent need. I had even called the prayer chain but still no one came. I managed to handle the immediate crisis on my own, but I could not seem to get past the hurt. Just when I thought I had put it behind me, something would happen to remind me of how let down I felt. The people I thought would be there for me had not been. At times the hurt felt like a weight.

During the months that followed God taught me several things. First, circumstances may not be exactly as we thought. Not long after the crisis I found out that the prayer chain had broken down that day. My request never got passed along. Second, I learned God's people are not perfect. I don't know why my church family didn't respond when they did find out about my circumstances. But all of us allow a myriad of things to pull us away from more important things. In fact, I began to wonder how many people I had hurt without realizing it. Third, God also showed me that I could be too sensitive. Later, when I finally discussed my feelings with a few friends, they were saddened, but surprised that I had been hurt. They had no idea the crisis situation had hit me that hard. I am usually a strong, "take care of things" kind of gal. My friends assumed I had everything under control. They were heartsick I had been hurt.

All this happened about six months before my mother-in-law died in that car accident. If I had allowed a hurt to take me away from God's church then, I would have missed His love and care in the midst of a much deeper need. Again, I don't know the depth of your hurt, but unless you move past it and reconnect with a church you will miss out on so much God wants to do in and through you. Part of that reconnection may involve being honest about your hurt. Because I humbly shared my hurt feelings, my friends knew that I was open to their help and encouragement. The next time my family needed help, they met every need.

God's people may be imperfect, but the church is God's chosen vehicle to do much of His work on earth. The local church is the best place to find love, encouragement, and strength as you follow Christ. The local church is the ideal place for you to discover all God has planned for you. It's the right place to fire up your flat faith. Fully connect, reconnect, or connect for the very first time.

Chapter 12

SHARE THE LOVE

Action #5: Participate in God's Saving Work

Our oldest daughter is expecting. This precious child will be our first grandbaby. The entire family is bubbling with excitement, eagerly anticipating the arrival of the new family member. Kelley and her husband, Jeremy, told us the news about four months ago. They gave us a photo of the two of them holding up a sign that reads "Baby Irwin, arriving March!" I framed it and put it on the kitchen counter. Every time I see the photo I want to do a little happy dance.

Kelley keeps us informed about her health and the baby's progress. She struggled with all-day morning sickness for the first three months. Now she's feeling good and really enjoys feeling the baby's activity. The first ultrasound revealed a healthy baby. The second ultrasound revealed a healthy baby boy!

Having a new baby join our family is not just exciting, it's also miraculous. Only God can create life. Only God can form my grandson's little body just the way He wants it. Even now, God is growing and shaping him in his mother's womb to prepare him to join our family. His birthday will be a day of celebration and joy. We will welcome our grandson and we will praise God for the miracle He has accomplished.

A baby's birth is a miracle of God that brings joy and excitement. A spiritual birth is also a miracle of God that should cause us to rejoice. Only God can bring life to a sin-dead soul. Scripture tells us that heaven rejoices when a sinner repents and turns to God (Luke 15:7). Do you rejoice when someone comes to Christ for the first time? When was the last time you got to help "deliver" a new Christian? If your faith feels flat and dry, one of the best ways to ignite a passion for Christ is to join God in His miraculous work of spiritual rebirth. In this chapter we will review the exciting good news and discuss ways we can fire up our faith by spreading God's love.

God's Message of Love

> *For God so loved the world, that he gave his only Son, that whoever believes in him should not perish but have eternal life. For God did not send his Son into the world to condemn the world, but in order that the world might be saved through him. Whoever believes in him is not condemned, but whoever does not believe is condemned already, because he has not believed in the name of the only Son of God* (John 3:16–18 ESV).

Think about your family, friends, neighbors, and co-workers who don't have a relationship with Jesus. They are in a state of eternal condemnation (John 3:18). Just like the rest of us, they have sinned and fall short of God's perfect standard (Romans 3:23). Their sin has earned the wage of spiritual death and separation from God (Romans 6:23). Without Christ, they will remain alienated from God with no hope for eternity (Ephesians 2:12) unless God saves them.

God desires for all people to come to salvation (2 Peter 3:9). Jesus' death is sufficient for the sins of the entire world. For whoever calls on the name of the Lord will be saved. But they cannot call on Him unless they believe. And they cannot believe in Him unless they hear about Him. And they will not hear about Him unless someone tells them (Romans 10:13–14).

Think about it. How would you feel if that family member you've been praying for 20 years accepted Jesus? What would it do to your faith if that neighbor who openly scorned Christ was radically saved? Witnessing these kinds of miracles from the sidelines can rejuvenate a tired faith. Participating with God can fan the sputtering flames of our faith into a roaring fire.

In his book *Spiritual Disciplines for the Christian Life,* author Donald Whitney writes, "Only the sheer rapture of being lost in the worship of God is as exhilarating and intoxicating as telling someone about Jesus Christ."[1] I agree. In chapter 6, I told you about the unique teaching ministry for which God equipped me. Those years of teaching the Bible to spiritual seekers have been some of the most exciting and rewarding of my Christian life. God allowed me to have a front row seat while He worked one miracle after another. I witnessed the opening of spiritual eyes. I got to see people falling in love with Jesus. But I have a confession to make.

Tight-lipped

I find it easier to share the gospel when God drops people in my lap at church than when I'm going about my daily life. I have to remind myself to keep my eyes open for opportunities. I must purposefully work to notice the needs of others rather than staying inwardly focused. When I do, I experience God's pleasure and presence. When I don't, I miss out on the joy of watching Him work. Unfortunately, many of us often miss out on this thrill because we don't verbally share our faith with others like we could. What are we waiting for?

We have the greatest news in the history of the world. The gospel message is the "power of God for salvation to everyone who believes" (Romans 1:16 ESV). Our lost family, friends, neighbors, and co-workers can be rescued from eternal condemnation by the power of this message. So, why do we hoard it? Why aren't we sharing it with everyone we encounter? In fact, why aren't we going out of our way to tell them?

I've heard—and given—many reasons for keeping silent about the good news of Jesus. But a handful pop up again and again. See if you recognize any of these:

- I don't know how.
- Evangelism is not my spiritual gift.
- They won't listen to me.
- My lifestyle is my witness.
- I'm afraid of how they'll respond.

Let's briefly tackle each of these reasons. First, many Christians feel ill-equipped to share the gospel. You can fix this quickly and easily. Many great resources exist to help Christians learn how to tell others why they need Jesus as their Savior. In fact, appendix 1 in the back of this book is a great place to start. It includes everything you need to share the gospel. Or learn how to use the "Roman Road." With just a few short verses from the Book of Romans you can show someone her or his need for a Savior and how to accept Jesus. As long as you communicate the essential elements of God's salvation, you are sharing the gospel.

Another reason some Christians give for not sharing their faith is a lack of "gifting." In a 2009 survey on spiritual gifts, the Barna Group reported that just 1 percent of Christian adults claim to have the gift of evangelism. That percentage reflects a 75 percent drop since a similar survey in 1995. Based on the data, the report concludes, "While the Bible never suggests that one must possess this gift in order to share the gospel, the depressed proportion of believers who identify with that gift reflects the stalled growth of the Christian body in America."[2]

Some Christians erroneously believe that since evangelism is a spiritual gift, only those with that gift are expected to evangelize. While not all Christians are gifted and called to an evangelism ministry, Jesus did command all Christians to witness (Matthew 28:19–20; Mark 16:15; John 20:21; Acts 1:8). You have a unique audience. No other Christian has exactly the same relationships you have. God has you where He wants you to share the message of Jesus with the people in your sphere of influence.

A third reason Christians give for not testifying to the grace and mercy of God is that people won't listen to them. Christians think that the lost people they know will not want to hear the gospel message from them. But a 2004 survey by the Barna Group shows the opposite to be true. By far, adults who accept Jesus, do so most often through personal relationships. More than 40 percent respond to the gospel message offered by a friend or relative. Comparatively, 14 percent receive Christ through mass media, 14 percent at a live event, and just 10 percent through a minister.[3]

Adults respond to the gospel best when it's given by someone with which they have a relationship. That fact alone should encourage us to talk about Jesus with everyone we know. No, they won't all accept the message, but God controls that anyway. We're simply commanded to tell. And those that do receive Christ . . . well, glory hallelujah!

The reason I probably hear the most for not actually speaking the words of life to others is "my lifestyle is my witness." Our lifestyle should absolutely reflect God to others. But it must not and cannot be our only witness. I've known a lot of morally upright people who did not have a personal relationship with Jesus Christ. A godly life without a verbal witness does not introduce people to Jesus. A verbal witness without a godly life is hypocritical and meaningless. But a verbal testimony to Christ proven with a godly life is a powerful witness. We need both to truly make an impact.

My friend Lisa beautifully combines a verbal witness with a godly lifestyle. In fact, telling others about Jesus is thickly woven into the fabric of Lisa's life and style. Wherever she goes she tells people about the goodness of God. Whoever Lisa meets she tells them about the life Jesus offers. Her witness is not forced or mechanical. She loves Jesus, and she loves people, and she gets joy from bringing the two together. She wants others to know the Jesus she loves.

I want to be like Lisa. But, as I told you earlier, I often get wrapped up in my own little world. I forget that there are people around me who are lost and headed to hell unless they receive Jesus Christ as their Lord and Savior. I must stay purposeful and disciplined in my witness. I regularly ask God to show me opportunities to share Christ, but then I must remember to watch for needs that Jesus can meet through me. When I'm obedient to take the opportunities and meet the needs, I'm blessed and my faith is fired up!

The last reason listed above that Christians give for not sharing their faith is fear. You know the feeling. Your palms get sweaty and your heart races. You wonder what will happen if you speak up and tell them about Jesus. What will they think about you? What will they say about Jesus? Most Christians, including me, struggle with the same thing. But lately, God has been reminding me of something much more important than what people will think about me: Where will they spend eternity? A moment of discomfort for me is nothing compared to the consequences of what they do with Jesus. Are you ready to speak up and experience the thrill of being right in the middle of God's activity?

Make a Connection

Remember, statistics show that adults positively respond to the gospel most often when shared by someone they know. That means establishing and nurturing healthy relationships is a vital first step in evangelism. However, we shouldn't treat people like spiritual conquests. They will know whether or not we really care about them, their lives, and their needs. They are also a bit wary of our beliefs, so we must earn their respect and the right to share with them.

Have you ever wondered what your non-Christian friends and neighbors think about you and your commitment to Christ? About ten years ago, I asked a group of brand-new believers what they thought about Christians before they found Jesus. The following *perceptions* were common to all of them:

- They think Christians spend far too much time at church. Non-Christians often see our commitment to church as all-consuming. They fear that if they start attending, they will lose time for their families and hobbies.

- They think our lives are full of "no" and "don't." Non-Christians often perceive Christianity to be too restrictive. They don't want to give up things they enjoy to become Christian.

- They think we judge them. Our non-Christian friends may notice that our lifestyles are different from theirs and conclude that we look down on them for their activities and behaviors.

- They are afraid we might confront them with Scripture. The chance that we may quote a Bible verse during a conversation makes some non-Christians break out in a cold sweat.

- They think we are very different. Our lifestyles often seem foreign to non-Christians, and they may feel that we have nothing in common with them.

Although these observations may not accurately describe most Christians, they do reveal what many nonbelievers assume is true. Being aware of these assumptions will help us grow a relationship of respect and trust. Here are a few ways I've discovered to help overcome these roadblocks:

- Find common ground. Do you both have children in a soccer league? Do you both love snow-skiing? Connections like these make you more of a real person to non-Christians.
- Don't try to do the Holy Spirit's job. He is the One who convicts people of sin and brings them to repentance. If we try to change people's behavior, we will only push them away. Our job is to be their friend and tell them about Jesus. Leave the rest up to God.
- Be fun and exciting. Show them that Christians are not automatically stuffy and boring. We love to laugh and have fun just like they do. For instance, invite them to your annual Super Bowl party or Hawaiian luau.
- Be open and honest. Share your life with them, including your doubts and failures. Christianity is about real people living a real, sometimes messy faith.
- Keep praying. Constantly ask God to make you sensitive to when and how to share your faith. Ask Him to help you see their needs and know how to meet them.

Relationships take time to develop. We have to be diligent and consistent to build respect and trust with our non-Christian friends and neighbors. But when that's established, they will be much more willing to hear what we have to say about Jesus.

Time to Share

Once you've developed the relationship, now what? How do you start? What do you say? First, listen for the moments God provides to begin spiritual conversations. Watch for that activity that only God can do. A non-Christian friend may wonder how you can be so peaceful in the midst of a difficult situation. An unbelieving family member may ask you to pray for them. A neighbor may express concern about the future. All of these possible scenarios are God-given opportunities for faith-based dialogue. Be sensitive to the leading of the Holy Spirit. Don't make them too uncomfortable. You want to keep the door open for future conversation. Initial faith talks don't usually provide the opportunity to give the entire plan of salvation — of course, God can orchestrate it that way.

Next, be sensitive about how you share spiritual things. Make sure your "delivery" matches the message. A couple of weeks ago, Wayne and I tried a new restaurant. The food was delicious and well-priced. But I don't know if we will eat there again because the service was terrible. The waitress had trouble taking our order. My food came in a decent amount of time but Wayne's didn't come for another 20 minutes. We weren't the only ones having problems. We could hear complaints coming from all over the restaurant.

We Christians have the message of life and death. So why aren't more people listening? People reject Jesus for many reasons, but sometimes the problem is the "service." Often we fail to take advantage of the opportunities God gives us. Sometimes, we witness with a self-righteous attitude. And other times, our lives contradict the message.

Peter spoke directly to this issue:

> *But in your hearts set apart Christ as Lord. Always*
> *be prepared to give an answer to everyone who asks*
> *you to give the reason for the hope that you have. But*
> *do this with gentleness and respect, keeping a clear*
> *conscience, so that those who speak maliciously*
> *against your good behavior in Christ may be ashamed*
> *of their slander.* (1 Peter 4:15–16).

Peter gave us some godly advice about how to tell others about
Jesus. First, if we make Jesus our priority, we will be watching
for opportunities to witness. Second, we can always be ready by
learning how to share the gospel now. Third, we can avoid self-
righteousness and speak with grace if we remember that we are
sinners saved by grace. Fourth, by living a godly life we will help
the cause of Christ and not harm it.

Next, be ready to share what Jesus has done for you personally.
In John chapter 9, Jesus healed a man who had been blind from
birth. It caused so many questions in the community that his
neighbors brought the man to the Pharisees. They pressed him
to give them information about Jesus, the Healer. He could not
answer all their questions, but they could not deny what Jesus had
done for him. "One thing I do know. I was blind but now I see!"
(John 9:25).

Your personal testimony—how Jesus has worked in your
life—is a real-life example of the power of the gospel message.
When you share what Jesus can do for them, your own life will be
proof of how He works. But don't fall into the trap of sharing your
own story without sharing Jesus' story. Non-Christians must hear
both. Give the gospel message clearly and make sure you give them
an opportunity to respond. Just remember to leave the results to
God. God has made it clear to me that only He can save.

A friend of mine from church once asked me to lead a Bible study in her home. She had developed relationships with several non-Christian women who were interested in studying the Bible and learning more about Christianity. It was a great arrangement: I would teach and she would provide the snacks. Every Tuesday night six or seven of us would gather, eat something chocolate, and discuss spiritual truth.

One of these ladies was also studying with a group of Jehovah's Witnesses on Thursday nights. Karen clearly knew she needed something she didn't have. I prayed constantly that God would give her a clear understanding of His truth. Every Tuesday night felt like a spiritual battle. Karen would ask me about things the Jehovah's Witnesses told her, and I would show her God's truth from Scripture. Week after week I prayed. Week after week she returned to our study filled with more false teaching. Week after week I worked to combat the lies with God's truth.

By the time our study group ended Karen had chosen to join the Jehovah's Witnesses. I was crushed and so worried that I had somehow failed both her and God. Then a wise, godly friend reminded me that I have no power to save. Only God can do that. Karen's — and anyone's — salvation begins and ends with God. He just asks that we are available and obedient to tell.

I told you this story for two reasons. First, to remind you that God only expects us to tell others about Jesus graciously. He is responsible for the outcome. And second, to emphasize that even though Karen did not accept Christ as her Savior, God still used the experience to grow and energize my faith. Both my prayer life and my dependence on God escalated during that time. And the echoes remain. I still pray for Karen. I am convinced that God is not finished yet.

Don't Hold Back

If you want to get excited about your faith, then share Christ with someone who needs to know Him. Only God can create interest in Jesus, provide spiritual understanding, and give eternal salvation. When you join Him in these activities you will be on the front lines of faith. You will experience God's power and presence in the lives of others. Watching Him work to change someone's eternal destiny is a unique thrill that cannot be duplicated. Share the good news. Don't hold back.

PART FOUR:

FIRED UP

Chapter 13

NOT FOR SISSIES

What is it about a fire that so captures our attention? I've spent many nights sitting around a campfire staring into its depths, transfixed by the yellow to orange to red flames. Dancing and curling, the flames hungrily consume logs, branches, and twigs. (And yes, sometimes the fire consumes my marshmallow too.) As I watch, if the fire diminishes, instinctively I reach for another limb or just one more log to keep the fire burning brightly. I don't want the heat or the dance to die.

Every fire has a beginning, a point in time when spark first meets tinder. Tinder ignites and the flame spreads to kindling. Then soon larger pieces of combustible material are added to the small fire and it grows. Without this fuel, a fire will eventually burn itself out. Similarly, a fiery, passionate faith needs a continuous source of spiritual fuel to keep it burning. Otherwise, the flames shrink and our once vibrant faith cools to a dispassionate, common thing.

Together, we have explored five attitudes and five actions that act as spiritual fuel for our faith. When God puts spark to that fuel, our faith will burn bright and intense. If you've been a Christian for very long, you've probably considered many—and maybe all—of these truths. I had heard it all but still struggled with flat faith. I knew a lot of facts, but never allowed them to shape my faith. But when I finally reached a point of desperation—when I desired a passionate relationship with Jesus enough to risk obedience—then I actually began to apply those attitudes and actions to my life. Are you there? Are you ready to step out in obedience?

To experience a fiery faith, we must go beyond merely *knowing* about these attitudes and actions. We must humbly submit ourselves to their truth and then follow God in complete obedience. Although we talked specifically about obedience in chapter 10, every attitude and action we considered requires steps of obedience. Without obedience, these things will never affect our faith; they will remain strictly head knowledge.

Scripture reveals a close connection between our obedience and an intimate, passionate relationship with Jesus. Obedience keeps our faith burning strong. Jesus Himself said, "If you obey my commands, you will remain in my love, just as I have obeyed my Father's commands and remain in his love" (John 15:10). Obedience keeps the lines of communication open and fosters our dependence on God. Disobedience builds walls and cultivates stubborn independence from God.

I would love to say I always obey everything God says. Unfortunately, even when I know exactly what God wants me to do, I still sometimes rebelliously choose my own way. Why is that? Recently I heard Patsy Clairmont say something that I think explains it well. "Obeying God is simple. It just isn't always easy."

God does not hide His commands from us. He wants us to know His will. Scripture and the indwelling Holy Spirit clearly teach God's commands to His children. Yes, it's that simple. But, obedience often comes with a price. We may have to give up time, resources, or comfort. Obedience may mean ridicule, persecution, or endurance. Sometimes, I see the path of obedience, but balk because of some pain, hardship, or even simple inconvenience that walking that path may bring.

Stories of God's people who both knew and obeyed God's will fill the pages of Scripture and history. Their obedience and its results exemplifies passionate, fiery faith lived out in the real world. The Apostle Paul epitomizes this kind of faith. Because Paul obeyed, God used his life to impact the world for the kingdom of God.

Paul's Fire of Faith

In chapter 8, I told you how God impressed me with the need to memorize His Word. One of the first passages I committed to memory is from Paul's letter to the Christians in Philippi:

> But whatever was to my profit I now consider loss for the sake of Christ. What is more, I consider everything a loss compared to the surpassing greatness of knowing Christ Jesus my Lord, for whose sake I have lost all things. I consider them rubbish, that I may gain Christ and be found in him, not having a righteousness of my own that comes from the law, but that which is through faith in Christ — the righteousness that comes from God and is by faith. I want to know Christ and the power of his resurrection and the fellowship of sharing in his sufferings, becoming like him in his death, and so, somehow, to attain to the resurrection from the dead (Philippians 3:7–11).

Every time I read or quote these verses, Paul's passion for Christ overwhelms me. Paul's desire to know and experience his Savior intimately overshadowed all other needs and desires. Paul did not write these words for mere dramatic effect. Admiration from the

Philippians over his "spirituality" was not his intention. No, Paul meant every word.

Paul's writings reveal his passion for the Savior even 2,000 years after he penned them. Just imagine the zeal of his sermons and the intensity of his demeanor! In the classic book, *The Greatest Faith Ever Known,* authors Fulton Oursler and April Oursler Armstrong paint a physical portrait of our passionate apostle based on ancient writings and fourth century art. Paul is believed to have been less than five feet tall, but athletic and strong. Even in his early 30s he was balding and gray. Yet, just days after his dramatic conversion, his powerful teaching in the Damascus synagogue astonished and baffled the hearers (Acts 9:20–22). This physically unassuming man possessed a gigantic faith.

> What transformed Paul, bespelling his hearers, was his fire of faith, a zeal that flashed and flared in those enormous eyes that were like two draft windows in a human furnace. He who often conceded that his bearing was not impressive stood in the Damascus synagogue and impressed everyone within the sound of his voice, beginning there a ministry for Christ that was to last thirty-nine years.[1]

His passion for Christ, his "fire of faith," set the course of his life. Paul practiced risky obedience out of love for his Savior. No command was too burdensome, no call too dangerous, no sacrifice too much. Paul suffered imprisonments, beatings, and bandits. He endured hunger, sleepless nights, and homelessness. He survived a stoning, three shipwrecks, and a day in the open sea. (See 1 Corinthians 4:10–13; 2 Corinthians 6:3–10; 11:23–29).

Paul chose the "plenty" of knowing Christ over temporary, physical need. Paul learned contentment in every circumstance of life (Philippians 4:12–13) because no matter the earthly conditions, he always had Jesus. Jesus' presence and power strengthened him in hunger, comforted him in loneliness, and guided him in times of uncertainty. Paul did not hunger after the things of this world because his heart and mind were focused on eternity. Paul was able to follow Christ obediently no matter the cost because he was laying up "treasures in heaven" (Matthew 6:20).

From a Roman prison, in his last earthly days, Paul wrote the following words to Timothy:

> For I am already being poured out like a drink offering, and the time has come for my departure. I have fought the good fight, I have finished the race, I have kept the faith. Now there is in store for me the crown of righteousness, which the Lord, the righteous Judge, will award to me, but also to all who have longed for his appearing (2 Timothy 4:6–9).

Paul lived with an eternal perspective. He endured the consequences of full obedience to Christ on earth in order to enjoy benefits this world cannot offer. He willingly "lost all things" that he might "gain Christ." To Paul, the world's best and greatest was "loss compared to the surpassing greatness of knowing Christ Jesus."

Around A.D. 66, the Roman emperor Nero ordered Paul's execution. Paul, presumably in his early 60s, received the death penalty of a Roman citizen — beheading. Herbert Lockyer, in his book *All the Apostles of the Bible*, reflects on Paul's last moments.

> What a dark moment of pain and shock Paul endured as the axe fell, but what a thrill of light and joy must

have been his the very moment when, for the second time, he saw the radiant face and heard the gentle voice of Jesus of Nazareth! For him to live had been Christ; for him to die was gain, for death meant to be with Christ, and this was far better.[2]

Paul's fire of faith first ignited when he met the Lord Jesus on a dusty road to Damascus. Through the years, his obedience continued to add fuel to the fire. His lifelong, passionate pursuit was to know Christ. Yes, this passion brought him physical suffering and pain, but the joy of knowing Christ far outweighed his temporal discomfort. By the world's standards Paul was poor, but spiritually he was abundantly rich.

More Fiery Examples

God's Word shares the stories of countless men and women of God who experienced the overflowing, abundant life Christ promises us. Their lives were not necessarily easy, but their dynamic, effective faith kept them intimately close to their Creator. These vibrant souls reveal faith qualities many Christians long to possess today.

Noah — one of my faithful favorites — stands in stark contrast to Abraham's wife, Sarah. Sarah didn't trust God to fill her empty womb, but Noah invested everything in God's plan for a floating zoo to provide a future for mankind. Sarah heard God's plan then determined her own path. Noah saw God's blueprints for the ark and picked up a hammer.

Noah believed God's warning and stepped out in obedience. Unlike Sarah, Noah knew and trusted God's character. He knew God would do what He said He would do in the way He said He would do it. And Noah acted on that knowledge.

This kind of obedience is not developed overnight. Noah's full submission to God was a by-product of their ongoing relationship. The fertile soil of Noah's constant communion with God produced obedience in a difficult situation. Genesis 6:8–10 gives us a glimpse into Noah's close relationship with God.

Noah's "righteous and "blameless" life pleased God (Genesis 6:8–9). Obviously, Noah had a track record for obedience long before God put His plan of judgment in motion and called him to build a boat. Genesis also uses the phrase "walked with God" to describe the nature of Noah's fellowship with his Creator. Following and obeying God was the way of life for Noah. He did not simply practice religion, he lived his life in the context of a dependent relationship with God. Noah's illogical, ark-building flowed directly out of his passionate intimacy with God.

Just imagine the jeers from onlookers as Noah worked year after year on that huge boat. God's path for Noah was not easy, but the way was filled with adventure and affirmation. When God judged the earth's evil with a catastrophic flood, Noah and his family bobbed safely in the ark.

Rahab, whose story we read in the second chapter of Joshua, also demonstrated fiery faith through courageous obedience. When Israel's leader (Joshua) sent two spies into Jericho to assess the situation in preparation for attack, she risked everything to align herself with God and His people. Rahab did not foolishly jeopardize everything for a God she knew nothing about. His fearsome reputation had entered the Canaanite city long before the Israelite spies. Rahab's faith was built on the knowledge of God as He demonstrated His power on Israel's behalf (Joshua 2:8–13).

Rahab acted on her faith by hiding the spies and protecting them from discovery. This risky behavior could have cost her very life. But she feared the one true God more than she feared the leaders and residents of her own city. Rahab passionately chose sides based on the power of God. Not only did God spare her and her family's lives, He also included Rahab in His work in a most unusual and unexpected way. Rahab the Canaanite was in the bloodline of passionate King David and in the ancestry line of Jesus our Savior!

Let's consider one more example of fiery faith from Scripture. During Jesus' earthly ministry, a Canaanite mother begged Him to heal her daughter. It's not a long account. We are not even told her name. Yet, Jesus' description of her begs for our attention: "Woman, you have great faith! Your request has been granted" (Matthew 15:28).

This mother had "heard about" Jesus (Mark 7:25). She knew of His power to heal and His compassion for the weak. This knowledge fueled her faith. But, what quality made this woman's faith so extraordinary? Spiritual persistence. She persistently pursued what she knew to be true: Jesus had the power and authority to heal her daughter. When Jesus did not respond to her initial pleading, she persisted. When the disciples tried to send her away, she knelt before Jesus and beseeched His help again. Even when Jesus' initial words to her were discouraging, she continued to express her solid faith in Him. The result? "Her daughter was healed from that very hour" (Matthew 15:28).

Noah, Rahab, and the Canaanite mother. These three biblical characters demonstrated fiery faith in God in various ways:

- Noah trusted God and His Word, responding with complete obedience to a hard, illogical task.
- Rahab believed in God's power and chose to align herself fully with Him, risking everything in the process.
- The Canaanite mother persistently pursued a response from the God who could heal, pushing discouragement aside.

Not for Sissies

We can learn a lot from these faithful three. Did you notice that their lives were marked by struggle, difficulty, and tough decisions? Jesus never promised that the lives of His followers would be easy. He said that if we *love* Him, the world will *hate* us (see John 15:18–19). He said that His followers would have trouble in this world (see John 16:33). In fact, Jesus urged all who expressed a desire to follow Him to first count the cost (Luke 14:25–33). Following Jesus is costly. Discipleship demands obedience. Submission of our will to His. The laying down of our life and the taking up of His.

What does real discipleship have to do with firing up our flat faith? Everything. Living a life fully submitted to Christ is not easy, but it's worth it. Only in obedient submission can we fully experience the rich, intimate, and passionate relationship with Christ that's possible. Paul, Noah, Rahab, and the Canaanite woman yielded their way to God's way. Through the trials of obedience and persistence they gained God's blessings. Safe faith is flat and dry. Risky faith — faith that yields all to God — is ready to burn.

When God spoke to Noah, Noah trusted Him and obeyed. Noah could have come up with a lot of reasons to not follow God's instructions. Instead, Noah went for broke. He invested all he had in all he knew God to be. Noah's unquestionable trust and obedience resulted in protection and affirmation.

Like Noah, my fiery-faithed friend Jan also demonstrates trust in God and obedience to His call even when it's hard. About a year ago, when the music minister left Jan's church to obey His own call from God, the senior pastor asked Jan to be the interim music minister. Jan felt inadequate to fill this role. Although God gifted Jan with a beautiful voice and an incredible ear for music, Jan did not have any experience leading a worship team or a congregation:

At first, I told my pastor I couldn't do it. I "knew" the band members wouldn't respect me as the leader. I sing harmony—not lead! I can't even read music! Yet, even with all my excuses I knew all God wanted from me was my obedience. So I said "yes." The next thing I knew I was sitting in the middle of a pile of music, telling God I didn't even know how to put a worship service together. It was all too big for me—more than I could handle. I told God I couldn't do it without Him; He was going to have to do it through me. And He has! I keep obeying and leaning on Him and He just keeps doing the job He gave me.

God called Jan to a task she could not do herself. She lacked the experience and expertise that most churches look for in a music minister. Jan had plenty of logical reasons to refuse the ministry role. But one thing overrode all that logical reasoning. She knew God had asked her to do it. So, Jan responded with trust and obedience. She trusted God with the music theory, leadership challenges, time, and planning. Jan received the overwhelming blessings of seeing God work miraculously on her behalf and sensing His pleasure for her obedience.

Rahab risked everything to side with the all-powerful God. She chose Him over her people and her city. As a result, she and her family were saved and God used her in His glorious plan of salvation for all mankind. Rahab's risky obedience positioned her to be used by God in a way that affects us even today.

Five years ago, Pattie—like Rahab—risked everything to side with God. Initially, she balked when she believed God asked her to be a missionary in Sudan. Living in the bush to plant a church among an unreached people group was a drastically different way to serve God than Pattie was used to. She would have to give up the comforts of western civilization, learn a foreign language, and be separated from her family for long periods of time. Then God reminded Pattie of His power. Here's how she shared her experience with me:

> I started to see that God was big enough to do something exciting with me, something that seemed impossible. As I prayed, I knew He was calling me to go to Sudan. And I did, with no regrets. I learned that it's by God's power I am able to serve Him. I can't wait to see what fun and exciting adventure He has for me in the future. I know it will be a stretch, but I'm learning to trust Him with the unknown. Whatever He chooses to do with my life will be great! I'm just blessed that He lets me be part of it.

Pattie left everything she knew and obediently followed God all the way to Sudan. God blessed her risky obedience with the excitement of being in the center of His activity and allowed her to be a witness to His power. Pattie's obedience continued to fuel an already fired-up faith!

The Canaanite mother expected great things from God. She believed God could perform miracles and she persisted in her faith until she received one—her daughter was healed.

Fiery Faith for Today

Many of us who have struggled with flat faith, long to possess some of the passion for God we've witnessed in the lives of others. Don't give up! Be persistent and remember God is faithful. Also, keep in mind that even the most passionate Christians experience occasional seasons of spiritual dryness. I still have periods when I experience characteristics of my old faith patterns. When that happens, the first thing I do is double-check my level of obedience. "Is there some area where I have been less than fully obedient to God?" If so, I must obey. If that's not the problem, then I evaluate the other attitudes and actions we've considered. Sometimes God chooses to remain silent for a season. You can trust He is still with you. God's Word is clear that He will not leave His child. But He may want you to practice persistence in seeking Him. In that case, continue to focus on your relationship with Jesus until God once again touches the fuel with His spark.

What would a fired-up faith look like in our life today? Although certainly not a complete list of fiery faith characteristics, here's what we've seen in the lives of our biblical and contemporary examples:

- Deep longing for God
- Intense craving to be in His presence
- Awareness of God's activity
- Life characterized by corporate and personal worship
- Clinging dependence on God
- Thoughts often consumed with God
- Active, vital relationship with the Creator God that shapes daily life
- Full obedience birthed from trust in God's character
- Willingness to risk it all based on the reality of God's power
- Persistent pursuit of God's intervention grounded in miraculous expectations
- Excitement and anticipation about what God has in store

All of these characteristics are rooted in the nature of God. They depend solely on His character, power, and authority. We can risk obedience because our God is risk-worthy. We can fully trust Him with the outcome of our obedience. He can heal any hurt, ease any pain, and replace any loss. As Paul reminded us, compared to Christ, everything else is just rubbish. Yes, the stakes could be high, but the result of risky obedience is far greater. In his book *Radical,* author David Platt reflects Paul's sentiments, "Ultimately, Jesus is a reward worth risking everything to know, experience and enjoy."[3]

What are you willing to risk? How about convenience, comfort, and abundance? Yes, perhaps. What about relationships, financial security, or power? A bit more risky. Physical safety, family, or your very life? Extremely risky. Sometimes, I am far too quick to abandon obedience in favor of physical comfort and ease. Sometimes, my behavior proves that the temporal is more important to me than the eternal. Sometimes, friendship with the world wins out over intimacy with my Savior. Sometimes, I still experience the spiritual lows that most all Christians occasionally experience.

But then there are the glorious moments. Those moments when obedience to Christ fuels my faith. My humble submission to God fans the flames and my passion rises. Yes, the risk is great, but we have so much more to gain. Obedience—no matter the consequences—fuels a passion for Christ that will permeate every area of our lives. The temporal results of risky obedience will be just that—temporary. But the spiritual and eternal rewards will be overwhelmingly glorious.

Take the risk. Check your attitudes. Adjust your actions. Then step out in full obedience to the One who risked everything for you.

NOTES

CHAPTER 1

[1]http://dictionary.reference.com/browse/flat (accessed August 3, 2010).

CHAPTER 2

[1]http://www.wilderness-survival-skills.com/how-to-make-a-fire.html (accessed June 24, 2011).

[2]Henry T. Blackaby and Claude V. King, *Experiencing God: How to Live the Full Adventure of Knowing and Doing the Will of God* (Nashville: Broadman & Holman Publishers, 1994), 124.

[3]A. W. Tozer, *The Pursuit of God: The Human Thirst for the Divine* (Camp Hill: Wing Spread Publishers, 2006), 20.

CHAPTER 3

[1]Richard A. Swenson, MD, *Margin: Restoring Emotional, Physical, Financial, and Time Reserves to Overloaded Lives* (Colorado Springs: NavPress, 2004), 30.

[2]Ibid., 64–65.

CHAPTER 4

[1]Ted Olson, ChristianityToday.com, http://www.christianitytoday.com/ct/2002/jneweb-only/6-3-21.0.html (acccessed August 22, 2011).

[2]Stephen Tomkins, *A Short History of Christianity* (Grand Rapids: Eerdmans Publishing, 2005), 22.

[3]http://www.dictionary.reference.com/browse/surrender (accessed August 23, 2011).

[4]Oswald Chambers, *My Utmost for His Highest* (Grand Rapids: Discovery House Publishers, 1992), November 3.

[5]Lysa TerKeurst, *Made to Crave* (Grand Rapids: Zondervan, 2010), 15.

CHAPTER 5

[1]Wayne Grudem, *Systematic Theology: An Introduction to Biblical Doctrine* (Grand Rapids, MI: Zondervan, 1994), 490.

CHAPTER 6

[1]Henry T. Blackaby and Claude V. King, *Experiencing God: How to Live the Full Adventure of Knowing and Doing the Will of God* (Nashville: Broadman & Holman Publishers, 1994), 29.

[2]Rick Warren, *The Purpose Driven Life* (Grand Rapids: Zondervan, 2002), 236.

[3]Ibid., 241.

[4]Blackaby and King, *Experiencing God*, 123–24.

CHAPTER 7

[1]Dr. Helen Roseveare, *Living Holiness* (Great Britain: Christian Focus Publications, 1980), 34.

[2]Ibid., 37.

[3]David Platt, *Radical* (Colorado Springs: Multnomah Books, 2010), 50.

[4]Ibid., 179.

[5]Ibid., 47.

CHAPTER 8

[1]R. C. Sproul, *The Soul's Quest for God* (Phillipsburg: R & R Publishing, 2003), 21.

[2]Jerry Bridges, *Growing Your Faith* (Colorado Springs: NavPress, 2004), 61.

[3]John Piper, *Desiring God* (Colorado Springs: Multnomah Books, 1986), 146.

[4]Sproul, *The Soul's Quest for God*, 65.

[5]Daniel Rados, "The Good Book Business," *The New Yorker*, http://www.newyorker.com/archive/2006/12/18/061218fa_fact1?currentPage=all, December 16, 2006 (accessed October 2, 2010).

[6]Kathy Widenhouse, "Back to the Book," Christianity Today.com, http://www.christianity.com/Christian%20Living/Features/11622479/ (accessed October 2, 2010).

[7]Piper, *Desiring God*, 148.

[8]Donald S. Whitney, *Ten Questions to Diagnose Your Spiritual Health* (Colorado Springs: NavPress, 2001), 37.

[9]Ibid., 26–27.

CHAPTER 9

[1]Arthur John Gossip, *The Interpreter's Bible: Luke John,* vol. 8 (Nashville: Abingdon Press, 1952), 527.

[2]Wayne Grudem, *Systematic Theology: An Introduction to Biblical Doctrine* (Grand Rapids, MI: Zondervan, 1994), 1011.

[3]A. W. Tozer, *The Knowledge of the Holy* (San Francisco: Harper Collins, 1961), 11.

CHAPTER 10

[1]Dietrich Bonhoeffer, *The Cost of Discipleship* (New York: Simon & Schuster, 1959), 66–67.

[2]Connie Cavanaugh, *Following God One Yes at a Time* (Eugene: Harvest House, 2011), 80–81.

CHAPTER 11

[1]Henry Blackaby and Melvin D. Blackaby, *Experiencing God Together* (Nashville: Broadman & Holman Publishers, 2002), 8–9.

[2]Barna Group, "Unchurched Population Nears 100 Million in the U.S.," http://www.barna.org/barna-update/article/12-faithspirituality/107-unchurched-population-nears-100-million-in-the-us?q=church+attendance, March 19, 2007 (accessed November 9, 2011).

CHAPTER 12

[1]Donald S. Whitney, *Spiritual Disciplines for the Christian Life* (Colorado Springs: NavPress, 1991), 99.

[2]Barna Group, "Survey Describes the Spiritual Gifts that Christians Say They Have," http://www.barna.org/barna-update/article/12-faithspirituality/211-survey-describes-the-spiritual-gifts-that-christians-say-they-have?q=evangelism, February 9, 2009 (accessed November 14, 2010).

[3]Barna Group, "Evangelism Is Most Effective Among Kids," http://www.barna.org/barna-update/article/5-barna-update/196-evangelism-is-most-effective-among-kids, October 11, 2004 (accessed November, 14, 2011).

CHAPTER 13

[1]Fulton Oursler and April Oursler Armstrong, *The Greatest Faith Ever Known* (New York: Doubleday, 1953), 119.

[2]Herbert Lockyer, *All the Apostles of the Bible* (Grand Rapids: Zondervan, 1972), 256.

[3]David Platt, *Radical* (Colorado Springs: Multnomah Books, 2010), 183.

QUESTIONS FOR REFLECTION AND DISCUSSION

CHAPTER 1: FED UP

1. What adjectives would you use to describe your faith?
2. Which of the biblical examples do you most identify with and why?
3. Review the flat faith characteristics on page 23. In what ways does this list describe your faith?
4. What have you done in the past to try to build excitement and passion in your relationship with Jesus?

CHAPTER 2: GATHERING TINDER

1. What things would you say you have "longed for" over the years? What do you think created those particular cravings?
2. Has there ever been a time when you felt like you truly longed for God? How would you describe that longing?
3. Review the list of things that Scripture says only God can do on page 32. List some ways you've seen God working recently in the lives of people around you.
4. Recall some of your personal spiritual "tinder"—a few times in your past when you felt you experienced God's activity or presence in a special way.

CHAPTER 3: INSIDE OUT

1. Describe what it means to practice religion versus having a relationship with Jesus.
2. In what ways could our Western culture hinder people from entering into a true, saving relationship with Jesus?

3. How does the Bible describe the relationship between our faith and works?

4. What did you discover when you evaluated the way you spend your time?

5. Why does the chapter describe "abiding in Christ" (John 15) as the "sweet spot" of faith?

CHAPTER 4: WHO'S THE BOSS?

1. Describe the true, biblical picture of surrender and submission to Christ. (Refer to Paul's words in Galatians 2:20.)

2. How has our western culture's consumer mentality affected Christianity and the church?

3. Has a consumer mind-set affected your faith? In what ways?

4. What four marks of a true disciple did we see in Luke? How did Jesus promise to bless discipleship?

CHAPTER 5: CRAZY IN LOVE

1. Why did the woman who anointed Jesus' feet with perfume love Him so deeply?

2. What does your sin look like in the light of God's holiness?

3. Think about Christ's sacrificial death on the Cross. How does this act of grace and mercy impact you?

4. How could contemplating the forgiveness you have in Christ foster a greater love for Him?

CHAPTER 6: BEST-LAID PLANS

1. Why does the Bible say God created you? Does this truth surprise you? How is it different than what you've heard before?

2. What is the scope of God's purposes? What goal is He working toward?

3. How is joining God in His purposes different than carrying out your purposes for God?

4. Did you prayerfully consider how God has uniquely prepared you to join Him in His purposes? What insight did you gain?

CHAPTER 7: FROM HERE TO ETERNITY

1. Describe the difference between an eternal and a temporal perspective.
2. What are some things that have lasting or eternal value?
3. What does the Bible teach about trials in a Christian's life? How should we respond to trials?
4. How should eternity affect the way you use your resources?
5. What changes could you make in your life to live with more of an eternal perspective?

CHAPTER 8: FEAST ON THE WORD

1. How would you describe your current level of interaction with the Bible?
2. What does the Bible teach about itself? How should these truths impact the way you interact with it?
3. What are some ways God can bless us through the Bible?
4. Do you desire to read and study God's Word? What are some ways you can increase your desire for it?

CHAPTER 9: GIVING GOD HIS DUE

1. What does it mean to worship God?
2. Describe the current role of worship in your own life.
3. Why does God deserve our worship?
4. How can you foster worship in your life? How can deeper worship invigorate your faith?

CHAPTER 10: SPARKS OF OBEDIENCE

1. How does disobedience create distance between us and God?

2. In what ways does God bless obedience?
3. How can steps of obedience fire up a dry, flat faith?
4. What step of obedience is God prompting you to take today?

CHAPTER 11: FAMILY TIES

1. Are you currently connected to a local church in service and fellowship? If not, why not?
2. How is faith in Christ "communal"?
3. How does God use the local church to bless individual believers?
4. If you've been hurt in a church, how can you move past that hurt?
5. What is your responsibility to the local church?

CHAPTER 12: SHARE THE LOVE

1. How can an individual's salvation fire up our faith?
2. Do you struggle with talking to others about Jesus? If so, in what ways?
3. How would you answer the common reasons many Christians give for not verbally sharing their faith?
4. Think about a non-Christian you know. In what ways can you build a relationship with that person? Name some ways you can begin a spiritual conversation.
5. What would you tell that person about how Jesus has worked in your life?

CHAPTER 13: NOT FOR SISSIES

1. Why is fiery faith risky?
2. What did Paul's passionate zeal cost him? What did he gain?
3. Does "fiery faith" equate with physical comfort? Why or why not?
4. What do we experience when we completely yield to God and fully obey Him?
5. Are you ready to step out and experience fiery faith?

HOW TO HAVE A RELATIONSHIP WITH JESUS

Sin has broken our relationship with God and we are condemned to eternal death. But because He loves us, God sent Jesus to pay the penalty of our sins by His death on the Cross. Jesus' death and resurrection makes a way possible for us to have a relationship with God and to live—after this physical life—eternally with Him. This eternal life is a free gift of God's grace. However, it does not come to every person automatically:

We must accept this gift.
But, how do we do this?

1. You must admit you are a sinner. You must confess this to God and repent, turning from your sin to God. See Acts 3:19.
2. You must believe that Jesus is God's Son and trust Him as the Savior that paid for your sins on the Cross. See John 20:31.
3. You must believe that Jesus was resurrected and confess Him as Lord of your life. See Romans 10:9–10.

"Believe" means to "have faith in; to put trust in." Believing in Jesus is more than just intellectual acknowledgment. It means you turn your life over to His control and make Jesus your Lord.

Making Jesus your "Lord" means that you give up running your own life. See Galatians 2:20. It means that just like Jesus died on the Cross, you willingly "die" or give up any rights to your own life. You die to your old identity, including all your old values and practices. You turn your life over to Christ and let Him have control. You allow Him to reshape your life and your identity.

This is both an initial and continual surrender. When you give your life to Christ for the first time, the Holy Spirit comes into your life, giving you spiritual rebirth. Then you will begin to understand what it means to make Jesus Lord in a practical and actual way. As you grow spiritually, you will learn to give Jesus control of every area of your life — big and small. The more you surrender to Christ, the more He will live out His purposes through you. His purposes for your life include good works as you obediently follow His direction. (See Ephesians 2:10.)

This is what it means to be a Christian. Your spirit, once dead in sin, has been bought back to life by the blood of Christ. Have you accepted this gift and given your life to Him? If not, why not?

If you desire to become a Christian, to commit your life to Christ, you can do that right now. Just express your commitment to God through a simple, heartfelt prayer of faith.

SAMPLE PRAYER:
Lord, I know that I am a sinner. I believe that Jesus is Your Son who willingly died to pay for my sins. I accept Jesus into my life as my Savior and Lord. Please forgive my sin and give me eternal life. Help me to now live my life for You. Thank You, God! Amen.

If you have given your life to Jesus, please tell a Christian friend and ask them to help you get started in your new life. It would also be a blessing to me if you let me know about your decision.

Appendix 2:

RECOMMENDED STUDY HELPS

1. Compare several recent translations of the Bible — Read your passage of study in more than one translation and compare them for greater understanding. Some good ones to try:

    a. New International Version

    b. New American Standard Bible

    c. Amplified Bible

    d. English Standard Version

    e. New Living Translation

2. Exhaustive Concordance — If you don't have any other tool, you need to have this index of every word in the Bible. Get one that corresponds to your primary translation. Recommended:

    a. *The Strongest NIV Exhaustive Concordance*

3. Bible Dictionary — Explains many of the words, topics, customs, and traditions in the Bible. It also includes historical, geographical, cultural, and archeological information. A few to try:

    a. *Holman Illustrated Bible Dictionary*

    b. *Illustrated Bible Dictionary*

    c. *Tyndale Bible Dictionary*

    d. *Nelson's New Illustrated Bible Dictionary*

    e. *New International Bible Dictionary*

4. Topical Bible — Similar to a concordance but organizes by topic rather than words. A couple to try:

    a. *Nave's Topical Bible*

    b. *Zondervan NIV Nave's Topical Bible*

5. Bible Handbook—Combination of an encyclopedia and commentary in a concise form. It is arranged by Bible book and includes background notes, brief commentary, maps, charts, and more. Look for one of these:

  a. *Halley's Bible Handbook*

  b. *Holman Bible Handbook*

  c. *The New Unger's Bible Handbook*

6. Word Studies—Look up the original words and their meanings without knowing Greek or Hebrew. Here are a few resources:

  a. *Mounce's Compete Expository Dictionary of Old & New Testament Words*

  b. *The Complete Word Study New Testament,* by Spiros Zodhiates, AMG Publishers

  c. *The Complete Word Study Old Testament,* by Spiros Zodhiates, AMG Publishers

7. Commentaries—Biblical scholars interpret and explain a particular text of the Bible based on their study of the background, language, etc. Keep in mind these are written by humans and are not infallible. But here are some good ones to try:

  a. *Tyndale Concise Bible Commentary,* Robert B. Hughes and J. Carl Laney, Tyndale. Provides biblical scholarship and commentary on every passage of the Bible in a user-friendly format (One volume)

  b. *The IVP Bible Background Commentary: New Testament,* Craig S. Keener, Intervarsity Press

  c. *The IVP Bible Background Commentary: Old Testament,* Walton, Matthews & Chavalas, Intervarsity Press

  d. *The Expositor's Bible Commentary,* Zondervan, Set of 12 volumes covers the whole Bible

Books by
This Author

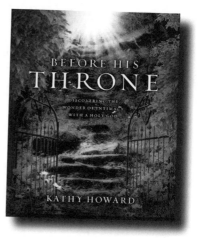

God's Truth Revealed
Biblical Foundations for the Christian Faith
ISBN-13: 978-1-59669-268-8
N094149 • $14.99

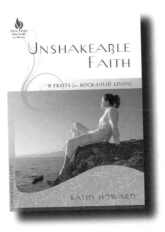

Unshakeable Faith
8 Traits for Rock-Solid Living
ISBN-13: 978-1-59669-297-8
N114134 • $8.99

Before His Throne
Discovering the Wonder of
Intimacy with a Holy God
ISBN-13: 978-1-59669-334-0
N124141 • $14.99

Available in
bookstores everywhere

NEW HOPE
PUBLISHERS
Gospel-Centered. Missions-Driven.

For information about these books or authors,
visit www.NewHopeDigital.com

Experience the free online Book Club Discussion Guide for *The Moses Quilt*.

Get more out of your reading experience at NewHopeDigital.com. If you've been blessed by this book, we would like to hear your story. The publisher and author welcome your comments and suggestions at: newhopereader@wmu.org.